365 UNPLUGGED
FAMILY FUN ACTIVITIES

365
Unplugged Family
Fun Activities

A Year's Worth of Ideas for
TV-Free, Video-Free, and
Computer Game–Free
Entertainment

Steve Bennett
Ruth Bennett

Da Capo
LIFE
LONG

A Member of the Perseus Books Group

Copyright © 2005 by Steve and Ruth Bennett

Illustrations by Ruth Bennett

Interior designed by Brent Wilcox
Set in 11 point Berkeley Book by the Perseus Books Group

Bennett, Steven J., 1951-
     365 unplugged family fun activities : a year's worth of ideas for TV-free, video-free, and computer game-free entertainment / Steve Bennett, Ruth Bennett.
          p.   cm.
     ISBN 0-7382-1000-5 (pbk. : alk. paper)
     1. Family recreation—Handbooks, manuals, etc.   2. Amusements—Handbooks, manuals, etc.   I. Title: Three hundred sixty-five unplugged family fun activities.   II. Bennett, Ruth (Ruth Loetterle)   III. Title.
     GV182.8.B46   2005
     790.1'91—dc22

                                                                    2004025373

First Da Capo Press edition 2005

Published by Da Capo Press
A member of the Perseus Books Group
www.dacapopress.com

1 2 3 4 5 6 7 8 9—08 07 06 05

Acknowledgments

As with all our work, first thanks go to our children, Noah and Audrey, who never cease to inspire and amaze us with their creativity. You've taught us invaluable lessons about the art and science of good-old-fashioned fun. Thanks, too, go to our editor, Marnie Cochran, for believing in our work and for her saintly patience—may you dazzle your kids with the ultimate Cereal Box Head!

Contents

OUT AND ABOUT

Things to Do Instead of . . .

Playing Handheld Games

ON THE ROAD

Things to Do Instead of . . .

Handheld Electronic Games
In-car Video

Introduction

Fifteen years ago we faced a parenting dilemma: how to handle television with our then two-year-old son, Noah. He hadn't seen much television, as we primarily used our set to watch rented videos after his bedtime. And we probably wouldn't have thought a whole lot about television were it not for the fact that Noah's coming of TV-watching age coincided with Sesame Street's twentieth anniversary. We were chagrined by the dearth of negative commentary about the venerable program, primarily how its fast-paced format was shrinking kids' attention spans. Hey, wasn't this supposed to be good for our children's brain development? About the same time, a flood of psychologists, psychiatrists, pediatricians, educators, sociologists, and others began weighing in on the larger TV problem, connecting the dots on the screen with alarming trends—decreasing ability to concentrate, increasing waist lines due to sedentary lifestyles and exposure to junk food ads, increased crime from exposure to violence, decreased racial tolerance, and worse.

Yikes! How much TV was too much TV? Was any of it any good? Any of it *not* harmful? Should we simply toss the one-eyed monster? Decree a TV-watching limit? Instead of formulating an official television policy, we conducted an experiment to see if we could generate so many fun alternatives that TV wouldn't be an issue. We relocated our nine-inch black and white set to the closet and moved the recycling bin into the playroom. Cardboard tubes, boxes, and paper bags became the stuff of treasure hunts and fanciful flights to distant galaxies. Plastic utensils and bits of yarn transformed into theatrical puppets that would have garnered a wink from the Bard himself. And junk mail became a rich source of images for comic books, story cards, and more fun stuff than you'd find in a well-stocked toy store.

The experiment worked. TV was always an option for Noah, but he rarely chose it since he was having too much fun with our goofy homespun activities. Ditto for our daughter, Audrey, who was born a year into the TV alternative program.

We subsequently published our ideas in a series of activity books that have sold about 1 million copies. Ironically, we often went on national television to show people how NOT to watch television. The hosts and guests in the audience treated us like anthropologists who had rediscovered an ancient ritual—parents playing with their kids!

Fast forward to 2004. Lots of things have changed since we began our experiment. Our diminutive TV came out of the closet and was replaced by a twenty-seven-inch color set (still puny by today's standards). Our son, now seventeen, and our daughter, now fourteen, flip on the set when they want to watch a program. They're fans of *The Simpsons* and a couple of other shows (so are we). And they enjoy renting DVDs several times a month (same for us). The key is, they have something far more meaningful and valuable than a perfect "no-TV record": they're in total control of the "off switch" and can regulate their own television consumption. As a result, TV has never been a battle area for us or for them. We think this is a good thing that will help them navigate well through other areas of their lives, too.

We also think that it's especially important for today's parents of young children to teach self-regulation with regards to electronic media. As we sail deeper into the twenty-first century, electronic media will become even more pervasive and entrenched in our family lives. The Internet has eclipsed TV watching and brings with it a gaggle of new problems. Handheld electronic devices are everywhere, from game machines to phones with gaming software. In-car video systems have brought the electronic hearth with us wherever we travel. It seems as if there's no escape, no time to kick back with your kids and enjoy small moments without help from the media networks and entertainment industry.

This book is designed to help you reclaim those moments and to regain control of the "off" switch. You don't need a particular orientation towards technology to use it— just a yearning to engage your kids and show them alternatives to screens big and small. You can put our ideas to work side by side with programs and games that you find worthwhile and/or acceptable. We've never advocated tossing your TV or any other electronic device (don't pitch the boxes and foam packing either—they're great for all kinds of activities). And we've never recommended adhering to a prescribed regimen of specific shows, software, Web sites, or anything else. Parents need to make their own decisions about how much digital input is enough and what content supports the values they want their children to uphold.

That said, there is one basic belief that's cast in stone for us, one that we hope you'll adopt as well. And while it may seem counterintuitive in a world where kids grow up so fast and seem to be under the complete sway of their peers and the popular media, scads of research support the idea that *parents are still the most important people in their children's lives!* That's not only amazing and hopeful, but it means that *any* time you can devote to playing with your kids will have incalculable benefits for you and for them. Even eight-year-olds can be persuaded to abandon TV watching or other electronic pursuits in favor of a good round of "bocce socks"—if you're involved in the game. So with that in mind, we're pleased to provide you with 365 unplugged activities you can do with your kids at home, when you're out and about, or when you're on the road for vacation or other travel. You'll find plenty of alternatives to the TV, computer, handheld games, in-car video, and other forms of techno-entertainment. Before you dive in, though, please read the following notes about the book and the activities, so you'll get the most out of our ideas.

What You'll Need

When materials are required for an activity, you can usually find them in your kitchen, recycling bin, broom closet, or desk. Even so, you might want to start an "Activity Chest" that contains a good supply of the materials most commonly used in this book. With these raw materials on hand, you'll be able to instantly coordinate a variety of on-the-spot activities. Make sure you've got a stock of:

- Toilet paper, paper towel, and wrapping paper tubes

- Plastic containers, tubs, bottles, milk jugs, milk cartons, etc.
- Scrap aluminum foil
- Packing materials such as hard foam and peanuts (these activities are a great way to breathe new life into hard-to-recycle items)
- A supply of cardboard boxes of various sizes, some cut into sheets and some intact
- Magazines, newspapers, junk mail, catalogs, and other photo sources

In addition, when art supplies are cited as requirements in the activities, here are some of the things you'll need:

- A good stock of coloring and painting materials, including colored pencils, crayons, nontoxic markers, tempera paint, and brushes
- Nontoxic glue or double-stick tape
- Large sheets of posterboard
- Drawing and construction paper
- Clear adhesive covering, such as ConTact brand
- Scraps of felt, yarn, ribbon, and other miscellaneous odds and ends

Finally, to do some of the indoor sports activities, you'll want to have foam balls, small rubber balls, and Ping-Pong balls on hand. A few of the activities for older kids also require marbles and balloons (see safety note below). And for activities requiring a tape recorder, you'll want to have some blank cassettes and earth-friendly rechargeable batteries.

Safety Issues

Common sense is the key to fun and safe activities: Just apply whatever safety rules you already have in your house for games and projects that involve cutting, gluing, and painting. Still, we want to stress that some of the activities use items and materials not appropriate for small children, such as marbles, coins, balloons, and small objects that can represent a hazard if swallowed. These activities are marked with an adult-supervision reminder. When you're playing a game or doing an activity with an older child, keep a watchful eye on toddlers who might find the materials tempting morsels.

Curbing Competition

Finally, a note on competition for group activities. We always suggest minimizing the competitive aspect of activities, especially for younger children; they'll have plenty of time outside your home to learn how to jockey to be the "firstest" or the "bestest" or to have the "mostest." For some children, competition can add a nasty edge to otherwise enjoyable games. To downplay competition, encourage kids to try to top their own previous scores rather than yours, a sibling's, or a friend's. To this end, you might want to start a book of personal records and achievements. You might also want to redirect competitive play to cooperative effort whenever possible so that your kids direct their pent-up energy toward a shared goal rather than at each other. Of course, some games, by definition, require a winner. But you can still stress the fact that everyone who plays is a winner and that the object is for everyone to have fun.

INTRODUCTION

.... xxi

Which brings us to a final point: Don't worry about doing the activities "right." As long as it's safe, anything goes! And go with your child's flow. Consider our activities to be springboards for creative fun and play. Encourage your child to invent his or her own rules; offer praise for devising interesting variations and for creating entirely new activities. Give yourself the freedom to be a child again, too—even if you've only got thirty minutes a day to engage in our unplugged activities, you'll find yourself connected to your kids in new and unexpected ways. And staying connected is what it's all about.

Steve Bennett
Ruth Loetterle Bennett
Cambridge, Massachusetts
July 2004

AT HOME

Things to Do Instead of . . .

Watching TV or Videos

Playing Computer or Video Games

Surfing the Net

Adventure Treks

Intrepid explorers have to know how to avoid dangers like boiling-hot lava flows, alligators, snakes, crevices, and quicksand. Choose your peril; your floor is now covered with it!

To escape the danger as well as the "cabin fever blues," your young adventurers need to place stepping stones across the hazards. The stepping stones can include towels, throw pillows, sheets of paper, old clothes, and sofa cushions. As the kids try to get around the house without touching the floor, they can extend their path by adding more stepping stones in strategic locations. They can also incorporate beds, chairs, and sofas as "solid ground."

Encourage your children to create an adventure story to go along with the game. Perhaps they're space explorers on a distant volcanic planet or naturalists in the alligator-infested swamps of the Everglades. Either way, they'd better try to make it safely back to their space-swamp vehicle (you might recognize it as a couch).

Whatever you do, don't fall in. . . .

Required:
Towels, sheets of paper, throw pillows, couch cushions, or old clothes

AT
HOME

Your kids can't wait until Halloween to turn into pumpkins? Here's a witches' brew of fun that you can stir up anytime.

Have your child decorate the house with Halloween "props" (including cardboard pumpkins, a "witch's" broom, etc.). Then, have your child help prepare special treats for an at-home "trick-or-treat" session (perhaps you can bake cookies together). When the treats are done or cooling, have each child make a personalized "goody bag"; pass out paper lunch bags and art supplies, tape, and safety scissors for the project.

Create costumes using materials from around the house or wear ready-made costumes from former Halloweens. Then send the Halloween troop off trick-or-treating to various locations in the house such as the kitchen and living room, where you can pass out approved goodies (and set guidelines for devouring them).

Remember to keep this off-season Halloween party at home; you wouldn't want to explain to the neighbors why you're dressed up as a talking kettle and your child is garbed as a teacup!

Required:

Cardboard, colored paper, art supplies, paper lunch bags, costume materials or ready-made costumes, treats

Anytime, Anyplace Spaceship

If the cost and inconvenience of space travel is getting you down, why not book a trip on a very private flying saucer owned and operated by your young child?

In this unplugged activity, you and your child can make a "cockpit" by affixing yogurt container tops and large jar tops to a piece of cardboard. (Or, if space and supplies are limited, your child can "fly" the saucer from imaginary controls.)

Choose a destination: perhaps another planet. Maybe an interesting part of planet Earth that you've had a hankering to visit.

Once you know where you're going, fasten your seat belt and take off. While traveling, have your child tell you about the route you're taking, the landmarks you're passing, time elapsed, weather and solar conditions, and so forth. And ask the person at the controls whether he or she has any ideas about the places you might see and things you might do once you land. After all, your pilot has likely flown this way many times before!

Required:

Cardboard, tape or glue, yogurt container tops, large jar tops

AT
HOME

Your kids can test their athletic prowess and accuracy in this traditional arcade game, which has been domesticated for home use.

Gather up a collection of targets: Toilet paper tubes, empty milk cartons, and empty cereal boxes work great. Next, supply each player with rolled-up socks, foam balls, or Ping-Pong balls. Pick a safe spot for your arcade, such as a long hallway free of breakables. Then, using a small table or flat chair as a platform, set up the targets. Put a belt or piece of string on the floor about ten feet away to mark the throwing line. The kids should decide how many throws each player gets to knock the target down.

Required:

Rolled up socks, foam balls, or Ping-Pong balls; toilet paper tubes, empty milk cartons, or empty cereal boxes

For variety, switch the target or the balls. Try making a pyramid of tubes and see who can knock them all down with the fewest throws.

Step up to the line! Everyone's a winner. Test your skill and maybe even win a giant stuffed animal . . .

Archie's Tractor

Here's an ingenious little mobile toy that Ruth's dad enjoyed during his childhood. It's strong enough to climb up a book, but it's not motorized.

Adult Supervision

First find a wooden spool and a bar of soap. Cut off a piece of soap about the size and shape of a Lifesaver candy. Remove the flammable end of a kitchen match (your job). Place the piece of soap on one end of the spool and thread a small rubber band through the hole in the soap and spool. Insert the matchstick through one end of the rubber band to keep it from pulling through (see "a").

On the other end of the spool, cut a long recess so that when a piece of toothpick (slightly less than the diameter of the spool) is laid across the hole and is inserted through the other end of the stretched rubber band, it won't rotate (see "b"). Fine-tune your machine by experimenting with different kinds of rubber bands.

Required:

Wooden thread spool, matchstick, toothpick, rubber band, soap

Adjust the matchstick so that part of it protrudes an inch *beyond* the edge of the spool. Use this end as a crank to wind the rubber band until it's taut, then place the "tractor" on the table and let it rip!

Audrey's Tic-Tac-Toe Game

What's the most exciting way to play tic-tac-toe? According to our daughter, Audrey, it's: Winner eats all!

Your kids can play this game of edible tic-tac-toe on a placemat or plate with clean Popsicle sticks or chopsticks. (You can play, too, while you cook; it's a great way to have fun while something is simmering or baking.) The sticks are used to form the traditional tic-tac-toe grid. For playing pieces, slice two different vegetables, say carrots and cucumbers (cut enough to play three or four games). The carrots represent the Xs, and the cucumbers the Os, or vice versa. Of course, both children can eat the pieces after a game; perhaps the winner gets to choose different vegetables that will be used as playing pieces for the next round.

Not only will your kids improve their tic-tac-toe technique and pass some enjoyable time while you're working on dinner, but they'll get a healthy snack in the process!

Required:

Popsicle sticks or chopsticks, vegetables

Audrey's Tic-Tac-Tongs

If you've saved a few playing pieces from Audrey's Tic-Tac-Toe game and are looking for a greater challenge, try this variation.

Make the tic-tac-toe grid as before with Popsicle sticks or chopsticks on a clean placemat, and give each child some vegetable playing pieces—carrots, celery, broccoli, representing Os and Xs. Now for the challenge: instead of using their fingers, the players use tongs (barbecue or salad) to move the pieces. Older kids can use chopsticks.

Play as usual, with the added twist that if a player drops a piece before moving it to the desired square, the other player gets an extra turn. Or for a really zany game, if a piece drops before reaching its target, place it in the square closest to where it lands and remove whatever piece was there. This can work either for or against the player. Hotshot players can take the ultimate tic-tac-tong test: moving pieces with their eyes closed!

Ready, set, grab those tongs!

Required:

Popsicle sticks or chopsticks, vegetables, tongs

Has your child read every book that his or her favorite author has written (or especially enjoyed a book by a particular writer)? Then perhaps your child would like to write the author a fan letter.

Your older child can write (or type) what he or she likes best about the author's work, feelings evoked by the book(s), lessons learned from reading the book(s), and so on. If your child has any suggestions for sequels, new endings, or characters, etc., he or she can include them as well. Your younger child might draw a picture about the book or dictate a letter to you or another "scribe."

When the letter is signed and sealed, mail it to the publisher (sometimes you'll find the address on the copyright page; otherwise, ask your librarian to see if he or she can find it for you). Publishers are usually able to forward mail to authors. Even if you don't get a response, your child will surely feel good about sharing creative thoughts and praise with someone who has been important in his or her life.

Required:

Writing supplies, envelope, postage stamp

Optional:

Computer or typewriter

Balloon Decathlon

There's nothing like a lot of colorful balloons to brighten up a gray day. Fill up a room with an assortment of balloons, then stage a balloon decathlon (remember, balloons can be a hazard for younger children). Try these "events" for starters:

Adult Supervision

- Keep as many balloons in the air as possible by batting or blowing at them.
- "Throw" balloons for distance.
- Have a "slow-motion" basket-shooting competition (a shopping bag can be the "hoop").
- Sponsor a "javelin-throwing contest" with long balloons.
- Have the athletes lie down and try to keep the balloons in the air with their feet.
- Use a wooden spoon or paper towel tube to keep the balloons in the air.
- Have the athletes walk across the room while balancing balloons on their heads or hands.

Required:
Balloons

And when the contest is over? See who can pick up and put away the most balloons in the shortest amount of time.

AT
HOME

10

Small Parts!

It's great fun to guess the number of jelly beans inside a glass jar. And with this carnival classic, you can quickly turn your busy kitchen into an arcade.

Your kids first fill a few see-through plastic storage containers or measuring cups with different items (dry navy beans, lentils, uncooked pasta, etc.). For very young children, keep the number of items in each container fewer than ten.

Next, everyone takes turns guessing how many items are in each container. After each player has guessed, the beans, noodles, or whatever are dumped into a clean bowl or onto a placemat and tallied. Older kids can be the official counters.

Required:

Clear plastic containers or measuring cups, dried beans or macaroni

When dinner's on the table, you can bring the rest of the family in on the game by passing the containers around and asking each person to make a guess. And if players are too good at the game? See if they can figure out how many grains of sugar are in the sugar bowl!

Beat the Clock

Time flies—especially when your kids are trying to see how many paper or plastic cups they can stack before an alarm goes off.

Adult Supervision

Break out your egg timer and try these:

- Stack-a-thon: See how many cups your kids can stack, placing a paper plate in between each, before the timer goes off. Then have everyone do the stacking with his or her eyes closed.
- Bop-a-thon: Make up a rhythm and see how many times each person can clap it off before the clock strikes zero.
- Sort-a-thon: Divvy up a collection of small items, then call out the category by which they are to be organized (for example, square, hard, smooth).
- Sort of a Sort-a-thon: Suggest a tongue twister (like "sort of a sort-a-thon") and see how many times your kids can say it without tripping over the words within the specified time.

Required:
Egg timer, paper or plastic cups, paper plates, common household objects

Finally, try hiding the alarm clock!

AT
HOME

If you're of a mind to do some major housecleaning, why not capture the great results on tape?

First, enlist the help of your young videographer to "shoot" various rooms and their particular cleaning challenges. As your child takes the camera from room to room, he or she can describe how things look in their "before" state and point out what needs to be done.

Put the camera aside temporarily and have your child help you put everything in shipshape form (a great fringe benefit of this activity). Then show off your handiwork on camera: Have your child tape each room again (preferably in the same order as before) and narrate all of the improvements that have been made (pillows plumped, rugs vacuumed, closets straightened, and so on).

Whew, what a difference there is between "before" and "after." Now, how long do you think your home will stay in its new state?

Required:

Video camera, nontoxic cleaning supplies

Extra, extra! Read all about it! Kids launch new media venture while parents cook supper! Dinner finished in record time!

Your kids can make their own headlines on a giant newspaper "printed" on your kitchen table. After covering the table with paper, your junior reporters begin writing about zany "news" events.

To get the general look of a newspaper, your kids should write their newspaper's name in large letters, as well as some headlines and columns. The stories can be about anything, but suggest that they start with fanciful food stories to tie into the dinner spirit. The lead article might be: "Giant Meatball from Mars Lands on Shadybrook Elementary School! Principal Says: 'We'll Cover It in Noodles!'" After writing the headlines in large letters, your kids can draw some pictures to illustrate the articles.

Required:

Paper or bags for covering table, art supplies

Dinnertime will become chuckle time as the family reads stories aloud; encourage everybody to pick up where the articles left off and continue the story lines.

OK, stop the presses . . . and pass the ketchup!

AT
HOME

14

Adult Supervision

Required:

Blindfold, socks, pots or bowls, hats, coats, gloves, coins

As kids, most of us played pin the tail on the donkey at birthday parties. But that's just one of many blindfold games that your child can do to pass the time during cabin-bound days (see next activity for more ideas).

Blindfold toss, for example, will challenge even the most athletically minded child. Place three or four pots or bowls on the floor and assign point values to each one. Blindfold your child and have him or her toss several rolled-up pairs of socks at the target containers. Then try it yourself. Perhaps the object is to get the most or least points (perhaps assign negative or "penalty" points to some containers) or to get all the socks in a bin of a certain color. It's harder than it sounds!

Once the tossing games are over, have your child keep the blindfold on, then try putting on a hat, coat, or glove (or tying his or her shoes). You try it, too.

Finally, older kids (and perhaps you) will enjoy trying to make change while wearing the blindfold. Oops, did you really mean to give away $1.50 in change for that $1 bill?

Blindfold Games Revisited

If your child enjoyed the games in the previous activity, these are sure to be a hit.

Adult Supervision

Put the blindfold on your child and break out the paper, crayons, and markers. Then let your child choose something to draw: perhaps a person, a landscape, an animal, or an object. As your child is creating the masterpiece, ask what part of the drawing he or she is working on and what colors he or she is using. You're bound to hear some amusing answers.

A variation of this activity is to call out shapes for your child to draw: For instance, draw a box inside a box inside a box or five interlocking circles. You can also call out elements of a picture: Draw a man balancing on a ball and holding his left arm in the air. Add a tree next to the man. Place a bird in the tree. A cloud in the sky. Who knows where the bird will wind up!

Required:
Blindfold, art supplies

Finally, try this one on your child: Have him or her draw a clock with the hands at, say, eight o'clock. Be realistic, though; if that happens to be bedtime, your child might have difficulty drawing it even without a blindfold.

AT HOME

Bocce is an old favorite played with one small target ball and four heavy wooden balls for each team. It's fun, but it could get to be a little noisy (not to mention damaging) if you try to play it in your house.

For a quieter version, which can be played individually or in teams in a hallway, have your children use rolled-up socks instead of the large wooden balls; a small hard rubber ball (squash ball or racquetball) can be the target.

To begin, have one player or team roll the target to the other end of the hall. Then, starting with the other player or team, take turns tossing the socks toward the target, the object being to place the socks as close as possible to the target without touching it. Players score one point for each of their sock tosses that is closer to the target than any of the opposing team's socks (if opposing socks are touching, then there are no points). One good strategy is to use a shot to try to knock the socks of the other team away from the target.

Now there's a game that's likely to knock your socks off!

Required:

Rolled-up socks, small hard rubber ball

Build an Animal

Kids love animals as much as they enjoy playing with empty containers, pots and pans, and utensils. Why not put it all together and have your kids create their own menagerie from objects in your kitchen? All they need are some items from your cupboards and their imagination.

Your children can make animals they know or create whole new species of their own just by stacking and arranging kitchen objects on the table. For example, an upside-down ice-cube tray can become the body for an alligator or dinosaur, with spice cans or boxes for legs, two spatulas for its open jaws, and a smooth butter knife for its tail.

Similarly, a round bowl or colander makes a great turtle shell. Just add a wooden spoon underneath the rim for a head. And a row of bowls or plastic containers can sure look like an oversized caterpillar (your kids might want to tape on straws for antennae).

Yikes! Watch out! That slithering thing with fourteen heads is getting awfully close to the stove!!!

Required:

Everyday kitchen items, bowls, plastic containers

Buzz Ball

Keeping several kids occupied while you're making dinner calls for some real juggling. Here's a way to get your kids juggling instead.

Two or more players gather in the kitchen and select an object to pass. An orange, potato, or apple will do (so will a small foam ball). Then establish some simple playing rules. For example, set a timer, then have your kids begin tossing the object to one another. The player holding the object when the buzzer goes off has to sit down. Reset the timer until only one person is left, then the game begins again.

Older kids can keep score. For example, the player holding the object when the buzzer goes off might get a point; after several rounds, the player with the fewest points wins. Or kids can play *kitchen:* A player gets a *k* the first time he or she is caught holding the object, an *i* the second time, and so on. When a player spells *kitchen,* he or she bows out.

This version of hot potato will keep kids entertained for a long time—and you don't even have to heat the spud.

Required:

Kitchen timer, ball

Caption (Mis)Matchup

Sure, we may *read* the newspaper every day, but how often do we pay close attention to the pictures?

Cut out some photographs from a recent newspaper or magazine, along with the captions. Select photos from across the publication, capturing everything from the news and local sections to sports and food. Snip off and save the captions, and you're ready for some great photo fun.

Spread out the photos, then read your child the captions, pausing to see if he or she can figure out which caption goes with which picture. You'll probably learn some surprising things about the world around you!

For an interesting variation, try reading the caption and having your child draw an appropriate picture. Then pull out the actual photo so your child can compare it with his or her drawing. Which one is a better fit?

Finally, cut up and recombine both the captions and the pictures and randomly reassemble them. Read 'em and weep with laughter!

Required:

Newspapers or magazines, scissors

Optional:

Pencil and paper

AT
HOME

What does your child want to be when he or she grows up? Here's how you can find out.

On slips of paper, write down various job titles (use your own, your spouse's, or a friend's for inspiration). Make sure you include a variety of jobs (and feel free to include such zany positions as dinosaur trainer, bungee jumper, and haystack builder). Fold the papers in half and put them into a bowl, paper bag, or hat. Pick a job title from the hat, then act out "a day at the workplace" and see if your child can guess which job you're portraying.

Encourage your child to ask questions that will help uncover the job title: "Do you work indoors or outdoors?" "Do you work alone or with others?" "Is any special equipment required to do your job?" Then reverse roles and see if you can figure out the job title your child has chosen.

So, find any interesting possibilities for a second career?

Required:

Writing supplies, bowl, paper bag or hat

The best thing about word games is that you can play along with your kids and still keep an eye on your cooking. Here's one that's sure to help your kids pass the time before supper.

Your child names a color, then you and he or she take turns naming representative foods. The color red, for example, might bring to mind "apple," "pomegranate," "rhubarb," and "radish." When all the colors are exhausted, you can use other categories, such as "sweet foods" or "foods that can only be eaten with a spoon."

You can also use non-food categories, such as kitchen gadgets, appliances, or other cooking-related items.

See who can come up with the most items in a category, the most unusual item, or even the most unusual category. To make the game even more exciting, try this rule: The first two examples you think of don't count!

Some cereals are more than nutritious; when they've gone stale, they still make great art materials. Here's a way your child can "recycle" old cereal while you go about your kitchen chores.

Provide a Q-Tip and some glue in a small dish or cup. Your child can make a food mosaic using the glue to affix different cereals to a piece of paper. You can also draw an outline of a picture, then have your child add the cereal to create interesting textures—fur for an animal, a thatched roof for a house, scales for a fish.

An older child can make an abstract cereal mosaic or a picture of animals, houses, people, or flowers. He or she might draw the picture first, or once the cereal is in place, use art supplies to fill in any missing details.

By the time dinner rolls around, the cereal art will be ready for the whole family to enjoy—without milk, of course!

Required:

Art supplies, old cereal, glue, cotton swab

Cereal Box Heads

Are your kids tired of looking at the same old pictures on the backs of their cereal boxes every morning? The usual clown and dinosaur faces can get a bit stale. Here's a great way for your children to pass some kitchen time and create a treat for tomorrow's breakfast.

Have your kids cover the front, back, and sides of a cereal box with plain paper or pieces of a brown paper bag. Then provide plenty of crayons, markers, pieces of scrap paper, scrap felt, cotton, various recycled materials, and glue so your kids can add funny faces. For example, they can use recycled plastic bottle caps and milk jug caps for eyes, a folded triangle of paper or cardboard for a nose, and sections of plastic lids for ears. Cotton from vitamin bottles can be added for tufts of hair or beards, and straws make for fine antennae (for alien faces, of course).

When the faces are complete, your cereal box artists can add descriptive or zany names to their creations. So don't be surprised if tomorrow morning someone asks you to please pass the Banana-Nose Flakes!

Required:

Cereal boxes (not empty), plain paper or brown paper bags, art supplies, straws, cotton, sewing scraps, recycled materials, glue

AT
HOME

There's nothing like a chef's hat and apron to help your child get into the spirit of kitchen play.

To make a hat, take a tea towel and a long piece of paper the length of the towel and six inches wide. Lay the paper on top of the towel, along one edge. Take the two aligned edges and fold them over two inches. Repeat one more time to create a flattened roll or band with one edge of the tea towel folded inside the paper band and the other edge extending above the band ten to twelve inches. Tape the band in a ring to fit around your child's head, then gather the free towel edge together with a rubber band (on the inside of the hat) so that it poufs like a chef's hat.

Required:

Two tea towels, sheet of heavy paper, ribbon, rubber band

To make an apron, simply lay a piece of ribbon across the top of a tea towel. The ribbon must be long enough to tie around your child's waist. Roll the top of the towel down several times, then tie the ribbon around your child; make sure it's comfortable yet tight enough so that the towel won't unroll.

Now your child is dressed for culinary action!

Chef's Surprise

What do you get when your child combines vegetable scraps, liquid from canned vegetables, and other cooking discards? Why, a recipe for great fun!

Provide a mixing bowl, large spoons, an unbreakable measuring cup with water, and other goodies for whipping up a "chef's surprise." Some food coloring will enhance the creation, as will flour, corn starch, or leftover tomato sauce.

You might also want to supply muffin tins—perhaps the chef's surprise is Cupcakes Grotesque, or a casserole dish, such as Monster Soufflé. (Perhaps restrict pouring operations to the sink, in case the surprise takes on a life of its own.)

Be sure to ask the name of the creation, as well as questions about its origins, nutritional qualities, and how it should be served.

Warning: This is meant to be done by professional kids only; don't try eating this at home!

Required:

Cooking scraps, unbreakable measuring cups, bowls, spoons, and other cooking gear

AT
HOME

You've probably never thought of your kitchen as Savile Row. Well, here's an activity tailor-made to keep your child busy creating while you're busy cooking.

On a table covered with a large sheet of paper, your child can draw life-size clothes—fit for a life-size paper doll.

First, he or she can lie on the paper (put it on the floor first) while you quickly trace his or her body. Once the outline is back on the table, your child can fill in the clothes. The attire can be as fanciful or as fancy as your child's imagination allows. What about a knight in shining silver armor? A princess at the royal ball? Or even a mermaid or a centaur?

Required:

Paper or bags for covering table, art supplies

Another alternative is to take a jacket, pair of pants, or some other article of clothing, lay it on the paper, and trace around it. Then your child can color in the clothes and cut them out. Or he or she can draw in a head, hands, feet, and other features to make a colorful paper person.

Of course, your designer can tape the clothing to him- or herself. Voilà! A walking, talking paper doll!

Coffee Filter Painting

A hot cup of coffee is often the best way to get the grown-ups going in the kitchen. With this fun painting idea, coffee *filters* will get your children going—and keep them entertained.

Because of their absorbency, coffee filters make an unusual painting surface for water colors—a single touch of the brush to the filter will produce a splash of color. Just set up your children with a few coffee filters and some water colors and watch their creativity perk up. Your kids can also use water with food coloring instead of paints.

You might also suggest while you're cooking that your children cut coffee filters into interesting shapes or glue two or more together. A flat-bottomed filter, for example, can be cut down along the side folds and opened to make a great butterfly. Your kids can also tape their creations to the kitchen window to create a stained-glass effect.

Required:

Coffee filters, water color paints or food coloring, brushes

When your children brew up this kind of fun, time in the kitchen won't just seem like the same old grind!

AT
HOME

This recipe for fun calls for one video camera, a pinch of imagination, and plenty of kids' favorite foods.

Have your children create a cooking show based on the preparation of their favorite meals. Topics include assembling the perfect taco, mastering the triple-decker peanut butter and jelly sandwich, proper placement of chips on the sandwich plate, and how to peel a hard-boiled egg.

Once your children have decided on a topic and planned their show, help them set up at a counter or table that's at a good height for them to work.

Required:

Video camera, cooking ingredients for favorite recipes

Encourage your children to give as detailed an explanation as possible in the presentation; they can pretend they're explaining the recipes to someone from another country or even another planet. Alternatively, your children can concoct ridiculous recipes out of real or imagined ingredients.

Step aside, Galloping Gourmet, here come the Catering Kids.

If your kids can't stand the heat, they can make their own pretend refrigerator to keep things cool—with your help.

Tape both ends of a large carton shut, then make a door by cutting along one of the solid sides at the top, bottom, and left (or right, depending on how your children want the door to open). To make a quick handle, cut a small slot near the edge of the door.

For shelving, take another empty box and cut pieces that will reach from one side of the fridge to the other. Have your kids help you tape those into place, then collect empty shoeboxes and other small cartons for use as crisper bins.

To add a modern touch, your kids can trace around a shoebox to make a rectangle on the door. Cut out the rectangle for them, then insert the shoebox into the hole so that the open side is flush with the door. Tape it in place and voilà: an ice and water dispenser!

Best of all, this modern convenience is ultra energy-efficient and frost free!

Required:

Large carton, medium box, empty shoeboxes, tape, art supplies

Adult Supervision

Don't toss those bottle caps in the trash. Your older kids can turn them into a high-action game while you cook.

Here's how the game works. Kids write a number on the inside of each bottle cap, or on a piece of paper glued inside the cap, then toss or flip the caps onto the floor. If the bottle cap lands face up, the player scores the point value written in the cap. If the cap lands face down, no score for that cap is recorded. Players toss the cap a predetermined number of times; the player with the highest score at the end wins.

Alternatively, kids can play to a set number of points—say, twenty-five. Or start with a number—fifty, for example—then subtract the points they score from their toss. The first player to reach zero wins.

Your kids might get so fond of this game that choosing between Count 'Em Bottle Caps and dessert may be a toss-up!

Required:
Bottle caps, writing supplies

Creature Dinner Party

What if your pet goldfish threw a party and everybody—all the other animals, that is—came?

As you prepare dinner, imagine with your child that one of your family pets, or another animal, is having a dinner party, and the two of you have been asked to plan the gala affair.

First, have your child make up a guest list. Perhaps Highway, the guppy, would like to ask Fish One, the goldfish, and the rest of the fish in your tank to the bash. And, for variety, Highway also wants to include non-fish creatures such as Charlotte and Emily (a couple of felines) and Hobbes and Meendrah (a hamster duo). Of course, other guests can include zoo and farm animals.

Then have your child create a menu with foods sure to be enjoyed by all the guests. Encourage your child to include a variety so that there's something for everybody, such as fish flakes, cat chow, and hamster nibbles.

Your child can also list decorations that would be appropriate for the party. Perhaps coral reefs would make the fish and the sea animals feel right at home!

Optional:
Writing materials

AT
HOME

Kids often have great powers of memory. And here's a way to prove it during a lull in your meal preparation.

Collect a handful of small objects—toys, cans or boxes of food, and so on—and line them up inside a cupboard. (Make sure your child doesn't see what you've gathered.) Open the cupboard door, then, after you close it, see if your child can recall all of the items you placed inside.

For a greater challenge, see if your child can recall the items in their correct order. Adjust the activity to your child's age by varying the number of items and/or viewing time. Be sure to switch places and have your child test your memory, too.

Required:

Household/food items

As a variation, locate duplicate sets of items. Place one set in a cupboard and give your child a quick peek, then see if he or she can place the duplicate items in an adjacent cupboard in the same order.

When the final game's over, try this challenge: See whether your child can remember how to put all the items back where they belong!

Delivery Truck

Wouldn't it be great if you had a delivery truck bring food to you as you need it? Well, you can, and your child can be in the driver's seat!

To make the "truck," your child will need a sturdy cardboard box that he or she covers with white paper. Your child can decorate the box to look like a food truck, or perhaps like a dish of food. He or she can even put an advertising banner on the side: "Eat at Mom's Kitchen. Great Food—No Prices."

After decorating the sides of the delivery truck, your child makes four wheels by gluing paper plates to the side of the box (not extending below the bottom edge of the sides). Finally, your kitchen helper attaches a string to the front of the truck so he or she can pull it from the pantry or the refrigerator to wherever you're working.

Organize the food you'll need on a reachable surface, then call out each item as you're ready for it. There's nothing like fresh ingredients to make your meal a smashing success!

Required:
Small cardboard box, paper plates, art supplies, string

AT
HOME

Imagine this: You and your child are marooned on a desert island. All you have are the clothes on your back, whatever materials you can find, and your wits. How will you survive?

First, you'll need a place to spend the night. Have your child help you build a shelter out of rocks and leaves (sofa cushions, towels, and so forth; see activity 57 for suggestions). When you get hungry, the two of you can search for fruit trees, roots, and berries (perhaps provide some actual food for the activity; all this play can build up quite an appetite). Or you can make fishing poles out of tree limbs and vines (string and a yardstick), bait the hooks with fruit or insects (rubber bands), and see what you can catch.

Required:

Sofa cushions and towels, string, yardstick, rubber bands, blocks

If you get cold, you can build a fire after you and your child collect a pile of wood (blocks). And, once the blaze is roaring, the two of you can plan enough exploration and imagination activities to keep you busy until help arrives.

Relax, civilization is just a search party away.

Design a Marble Race

All your kids need for a day at the races are some marbles and cardboard tubes. Use a hallway or room with a wooden or linoleum floor for the racetrack. Have your children hold one end of the cardboard tube in the air while keeping the other end on the floor to form a marble launching "jetway." Each player simply releases the marble at the top of the tube to send it on its way. (Supervise closely if young siblings are watching the play. Also, if young children are playing the game, try using tubes that are large enough to accommodate Ping-Pong balls.)

Adult Supervision

The simplest race is to see who can get a marble across a finish line first. Your children can make the race more challenging by including a simple target at the finish line (say, a small piece of folded paper standing on edge). Or, they can try to have their marble stop as close as possible to the finish line by raising or lowering the ends of their tubes to control the speed.

Players ready? Marbles ready? They're off!

Required:
Marbles (or Ping-Pong balls), cardboard tubes

Optional:
Paper or other targets

It's customary in our part of the world to remove your hat when you eat. We'll break with tradition for this activity and encourage kids to make hats for everyone to wear at the dinner table.

The simplest kind of hat to make is the "dunce" or cone-shaped party hat. Your kids simply roll up paper into a cone shape, tape, trim, and add a piece of string or elastic thread for a chin strap. Before they roll the paper, they can decorate the hats with pictures from food circulars, food catalogs, and the like. If your kids plan to draw pictures on their hats, unroll the trimmed paper, have them do their drawings, then reroll and tape the paper into a cone. Your young haberdashers can also decorate stocking and other hats by affixing pictures of food with masking tape rolled and flattened.

The best part of the hat making is that your kids don't need a special occasion for wearing them. Perhaps today is chili day, so everyone wears bean-decorated hats on their heads—or bean to bean, you might say!

Required:

Paper, art supplies, elastic thread or string, food circulars, masking tape

Optional:

Hats

Draw a Menu

Does anyone want to know what's for dinner? All they have to do is read the giant menu on your table!

Cover your kitchen table with paper, and provide markers and other art supplies. Then have your child "interview" you about tonight's meal so that he or she can write or draw the courses on the table. You might suggest that your child divide the menu into Appetizers, Entrees, Side Dishes, Desserts, and Beverages. A child with writing skills can list the items in each category; pre-readers can draw the dishes while you add the words. To add a zany element, your child can write in the price of each item and even make special "currency" for other family members to use.

When your child is done with the menu, you can leave it on the table for everyone to admire, or you might hang it on the refrigerator for other "patrons" to see.

For a final touch, how about adding this line at the bottom of the menu: Each patron is expected to tip the chef one hug!

Required:

Paper table covering, art supplies

AT
HOME

Here's how you can turn simple drawings into a fun group activity and good Rx for the "cabin fever blues."

Set up a table with a sheet of paper and a chair for each child and have plenty of markers or crayons on hand. Next, have your kids suggest enough drawing topics so that there's one for everybody. Label each sheet of drawing paper with a separate topic. (As an alternative to separate sheets, you can cover the entire table with one large sheet of paper.)

Once all the kids are ready with a blank sheet and a drawing topic, have them start drawing. After a short time (about one minute) have everyone stop drawing, move one seat to the right, and continue with the picture at that seat. Keep going until all the kids have contributed something to each drawing.

Required:

Art supplies

For a variation, you can give each child one or two markers so that they all have different colors, and have them keep their markers with them as they move. That way, they can look back at all the pictures and identify which part they added.

On your mark, get set, draw!

Drawing in Tandem

Are you on the same artistic wavelength as your child? Find out with this activity.

Supply yourself and your child with pieces of paper, as well as crayons, markers, or colored pencils. Find a place where the two of you can draw without seeing each other's paper, then take turns calling out shapes to be drawn. When you're finished, compare pictures, and see how alike or dissimilar they may be.

A variation on the activity entails combining shapes, objects, and colors. For instance, the following sequence of drawing tasks—"square," "green," "tree," "car," "circle," and "yellow"— might lead one person to draw a picture of a house with a green front lawn, a tree in front, a car parked in front of the house, and a yellow sun in the sky. The other person might have drawn a statue of a car on a pedestal next to a large green tree with a round brass plaque on the base.

Required:
Art supplies

Want to get real tricky? Toss in some abstract things to illustrate, such as "love," "happiness," and "fear." You might be surprised at the window this opens into your child's mind (and your own).

Clear adhesive covering is one of the greatest inventions of all time. Here are some ideas for its use that will allow you and your child to create useful items that will last for years.

Placemats.   Give your child some drawing paper and have him or her decorate each sheet (both sides) with food, flowers, or abstract designs. Label each placemat with a family member's name and cover the back and front with clear adhesive, ensuring that each has a complete seal.

Bookmark.   Cut drawing paper to size (say, eight inches by two inches). Then have your child decorate it with original art. Cover it with clear adhesive and punch a hole through the top. Thread a length of ribbon through the hole and hit the books!

Required:

Clear adhesive covering, art supplies

Pendants and Ornaments.   Cut circles, stars, hearts, and other shapes out of drawing paper or cardboard and decorate both sides. Apply clear adhesive covering, and tie a piece of string through a hole in the top. Voilà! A hanging masterpiece.

This doesn't even begin to cover the possibilities . . .

Earth to Space

If your child is planning to take off into space in the near future, why not capture your two-way radio transmissions on tape?

While your child is traveling, turn on the tape recorder and document all of your conversations with the junior astronaut. Find out whether the takeoff went smoothly, what your child sees out the windows, what he or she is wearing, and so on. Also, have your child tell you the spacecraft's destination and what he or she expects to find there.

When your child arrives, have him or her tell you all about the landing site: what the weather is like, whether there are any living creatures (perhaps your child can interview one), what kind of food there is to eat. Then contact your child again on his or her trip home; if possible, stay in touch until he or she lands safely.

Required:

Tape recorder

These taped conversations are the earthlings' only way of hearing about this space trip, so be sure the astronaut clearly transmits all the important news!

Small Parts!

Is your child a budding mathematical genius? Then why not help him or her make a macaroni abacus?

Use a shoebox as the frame. Punch eight holes in the box, four in each end, spaced evenly. Thread a string through the first bottom hole and knot it so that it can't slip out. Then thread nine pieces of macaroni through the string. Slip the string through the first top hole. Now weave the string through the remaining top and bottom holes, adding nine pieces of macaroni to each strand.

The first strand, starting from the right, represents the "ones" column; the second strand, the "tens"; the third, the "hundreds"; and the fourth strand represents the "thousands" column. Each piece of macaroni represents one digit, so that two pieces of macaroni in the second column equals "20," three pieces in the third column is "300," and so forth. Your child can use the abacus to do some low-tech mathematical computations by raising and lowering pieces of macaroni and "reading" the results.

So, what's a plateful of macaroni plus a ladleful of spaghetti sauce?

Required:

Shoebox, uncooked macaroni, string

Eggtropolis

Here's how your children can make a cityscape out of milk cartons, shoeboxes, and egg cartons (with holes in the top).

First, cut a sheet of poster board in half lengthwise and tape the ends together to create a backdrop for the city. Next, have your children create buildings out of the egg-carton tops (the holes are the windows) and various-sized boxes. Each one will be glued to the backdrop so only the front and sides show, and your children can use the cartons in different ways to create a variety of buildings.

Have your children draw or cut out pictures of people to place in windows in the buildings before they are glued down and use paint, colored paper, and other materials to decorate the surrounding structures.

As each building is completed, have your children affix it on the background. They can then add pictures from magazines and junk mailings to complete the scene, such as birds or airplanes above the buildings and people walking in front.

Sounds like a city planner's dream to us.

Required:
Egg cartons, small cartons, food boxes, scissors, art supplies, poster board, magazines, and other photo sources

44

Embossed pictures are an art form in themselves. With this activity, your child can emboss right in your kitchen without expensive printing gear.

Have your child draw or trace the outline of an animal, a car, a leaf, or a geometrical form on a piece of thick corrugated cardboard. The cardboard should be at least the same dimensions as the paper you'll be using, preferably an inch larger on each edge. Cut out the shape with a sharp knife (your job).

Now take a piece of white paper and mist it with a plant sprayer. Apply just enough water so that the paper is malleable (if it's too wet, it will fall apart).

Required:

Corrugated cardboard, white paper, towel, plant sprayer

Lay the cutout cardboard on a flat surface. Cover it with the paper and *gently* push it into the cutout, following the cut edge with your finger. Next, place several thicknesses of a cloth towel over the paper to absorb water. Place a heavy object on top so that the paper remains in the cutout as the water evaporates.

When the paper is dry, remove it from the cardboard and presto, an embossed piece of artwork that your child can turn into a greeting card or a piece of art suitable for framing.

If your home library doesn't yet include a book about your family, then why not have your child make one or more?

Your child can write a fictional story that includes all family members in the plot. Other characters, real or imaginary (such as friends, neighbors, pets), can also be woven into the narrative. Or your child can chronicle a family event that really happened (the birth of a younger sibling, moving to a new home, visiting out-of-state relatives).

In addition to (or instead of) writing a storybook, your child can create a reference book about your family. He or she might include information about each family member, such as likes and dislikes, accomplishments, academic record, best personality traits, and plans for the future.

Required:

Writing supplies, stapler, binder or report cover

Once your child's literary work is finished, arrange to have the whole family read it together. This is one book that will speak volumes.

Are you searching for a good, all-purpose repair shop? You need look no further than your own kitchen.

Gather a variety of "broken" child-safe objects (stuffed animals, lunchboxes, cardboard boxes masquerading as radios, toy cars, etc.). Include some of your cardboard-box appliances as well (see activities 29, 47, 83, 96, and 145).

Spread these out on your child's "workbench." Add a box of "tools" (kitchen implements, such as a potato masher, whisk, nutcracker, and the like). For heavy-duty repair jobs, you might also include protective gear: a pair of (used latex) gloves, sunglasses, a hat or helmet, an apron.

Required:

Kitchen implements, cardboard boxes, gloves, sunglasses, hat or helmet

Then tell your child what's wrong with each item, and while you're cooking, your child can fix the problem. You might want to check now and then to see how the repairs are going. During a lull in the cooking, the resident expert handyperson might need your help holding an item steady while he or she fine-tunes an adjustment screw with the whisk—we hear that whisk adjustments can be very delicate procedures!

Flash in the Pan

Rustling up some dinner in this hectic world makes the microwave a great helper. Here's a way for your kids to build their own play appliance.

A small carton, like a shoebox, works great as a microwave. All your child has to do to start is set the shoebox on its side. If he or she wants the door to swing open, just tape one end of the lid to the box. On the front of the lid, paste a piece of white paper, then have your child draw a window so everyone can "see" the food cooking inside the oven.

Next to the window, draw a time display, a touch pad, or any dials or switches your child wants. A small round plastic lid inside the box becomes a carousel. Your child can even personalize the microwave with a nameplate.

To cook up a short snack, kids can place some pretend food (crackers or cereal, actually) in a small bowl, put it in the microwave, and "zap" it for a minute or two. How about that—a snack in seconds, and no chance of overcooking the food!

Required:

Shoebox, small round plastic lid, tape or glue, art supplies, white paper

AT
HOME

Once your children whet their appetites with this floating numbers game, it's sure to be a big splash with them; all it takes is a large pan, some plastic lids, and a few kids full of giggles!

First, write numbers sequentially on lids from yogurt, margarine, or other containers, using an indelible marker. Or number the lids in pairs so every number appears on two lids. Next, fill a dishpan or casserole dish about halfway with water and set the lids afloat with the numbers facing down.

When the pan is afloat with lids, try a game like "floating concentration." Have your children turn over two lids at a time to try to find matching numbers. Another floating lid game involves trying to turn over the lids in sequence, starting with the lowest number. The first contestant keeps turning over lids until he or she gets a number out of sequence, at which point the lids are turned numbers down again, the pan stirred, and the next child tries his or her luck.

Splish splash—this is fun your kids can count on!

Required:

Container lids, indelible marker, large pan

Floating Targets

Small Parts!

Do your kids enjoy arcade-type tosses? If so, this activity will keep them busy while you go about your kitchen work.

Create a set of floating lids as described in activity 48. When the pan holding the lids (targets in this case) is ready—this time the numbers on the lids should be face up—pass out some dry pasta or beans (as tokens) and let the games begin!

Your kids can start off tossing the pasta or beans onto the lids to score points. Players can take turns, or one player tosses until he or she misses a target altogether, and the next player "steps up to the plate." Each child, or an older sibling with math skills, keeps the running total.

A variation on this game is to turn the lids face down and then toss the pasta or beans at the targets. When a player's token lands on a target, he or she turns the target over and notes the points.

For the ultimate challenge, players toss their tokens at the target with their eyes closed. Oops! Sorry about adding the navy bean to the chocolate cake!

Required:

Container lids, indelible marker, large pan, uncooked pasta or beans

AT
HOME

Here's a simple drawing project that will get kids to take a closer look at familiar surroundings: their dwelling.

All you need for this activity is a pencil, a ruler, and some paper (graph paper works best) on which your child can draw a map of the inside of the house or apartment.

First, have your child measure the length and width of each room by "kid steps," counting each complete pace (that is, left foot, right foot) as one step. Help pick a scale that allows for an entire floor of the house to be drawn on one sheet of paper (say, two squares on the graph paper are equal to one kid step). It's also helpful if your child draws each room as he or she measures it, rather than trying to do it from memory.

Required:

Writing supplies, ruler

When the floor plan is done, your child can draw in furniture and color each room to match the real thing. Don't forget to suggest adding the most important part of the house: the people who live there.

Folding Room Screen

This folding screen is something your kids will have fun making and using for a long time.

To make the basic screen, use three or four large pieces of heavy cardboard; the sides from an appliance box work very well. If the box is intact, cut open one corner so that the sides are still connected and fold it accordion-style so that it stands up. If your children are starting with separate pieces of cardboard, make connecting hinges with strips of duct tape.

Now you can have your children decorate their folding screen using paints, markers, and pictures clipped from magazines (depending on the type of decorations they chose to apply, your children may want to first cover the cardboard with sheets of paper more suitable for coloring).

When the screen is done, your children can use it to enclose a reading nook or perhaps to designate where the playroom ends and the shores of a getaway tropical island begin.

Required:

Cardboard, duct tape (if cardboard is separate sheets), art supplies, magazines and other picture sources, sheets of paper

AT HOME

Do your kids know the basic food groups?

Cover the table with a large sheet of paper and provide food circulars, boxes, labels, etc. Have your children use crayons or markers to draw a twisting pathway of squares, and then place pictures of each of the five food groups—Fats and Sweets, Milk, Meat, Vegetable/Fruit, and Bread/Cereal—at various intervals along the pathway. Be sure there's a variety of food pictures on the squares.

Next make a giant die by cutting off the lower portions of two quart-sized milk cartons, two and three quarters inches from the bottom. Slit the corners of one of the carton bottoms, then insert it into the other. Tape the bottoms together so they form a cube. Cover the cube with craft paper. Your children can affix pictures representing the food groups on five of the faces. One of the remaining faces can be a wild card—say, advance a token (a plastic tumbler) two squares—or a penalty roll—say, move back two spaces.

OK—roll me an eggplant!

Required:

Paper table covering, art supplies, food circulars and other photo sources, plastic tumblers, two one-quart cardboard milk cartons, tape

Foodcaster

Sports stars get play-by-play coverage when they perform—why not Mom and Dad when they're working in the kitchen?

All you need is a large spoon to turn your kitchen into a broadcast booth. Hand the spoon over to your kids, and suggest that they tell the "audience" what's going on in the kitchen. Sometimes it helps to give them a quick twenty-second demonstration—just hold the spoon in front of your face like an old-time microphone and start off your performance patter.

"It's a beautiful day here in Smith Kitchen Stadium," you might say if you want to give dinnertime a sports flavor. Or, if you prefer a newscaster, rather than a sportscaster, approach: "We're standing in the kitchen of the Smith family, waiting eagerly for the first reports of dinner." At this point, thrust the "microphone" toward your youngster and ask him or her to describe how they feel to be part of this momentous occasion.

Required:

Large spoon

It may not be NBC, but combining sports- and newscasting with dinnertime makes for hungry headlines!

All parents have heard the phrase "There's nothing to eat in this house" more times than they can count. But after playing this game, your kids will never be able to make that claim again!

The object of this word game is to make up recipes using non-food items. How about your son's right sneaker? Boil it for one hour, then add half a cup of baseball. For dessert, your daughter might bake an interesting stuffed-roller-skate pie.

Your kids can select the exact proportions and describe the best method of cooking. (Perhaps the sneakers peel more easily after being parboiled for five minutes. They also cook more evenly if you remove the laces.) Time before dinner will evaporate amid the chorus of yucks that greets every serving of Sneaker Stew and Flea Collar Salad.

Your kids might also want to think about the nutritional value of their meals. That Sneaker Stew, so loaded with a "nikezine," is bound to make everyone a world-class runner.

How would you like to enjoy an indoor beach party in the winter or any time of the year?

Of course, you'll want to dress appropriately, so have family members dig out and change into their bathing suits, hats, sunglasses, sandals, etc. Your child can help you gather supplies you'll need (blankets, a cooler, beach chairs) and spread them on the "shore."

Next, turn your playroom (or other room) into your own private "beach." You might display toy boats, hang up pictures of the ocean, or set up cardboard box "hot dog" or "ice-cream" stands (with your child as the vendor to serve refreshments). Party guests can enjoy games of indoor balloon volleyball (pass a balloon over a string tied between two chairs), "sand"-castle-building (using pails, shovels, and uncooked rice or small noodles contained in a dishpan), and perhaps even beach blanket bingo.

Your guests might be tempted to take a break from all the excitement and lie in the sun; after all, why wait until summertime to catch some rays?

Required:
Summer garb, blankets

Optional:
Cardboard boxes, refreshments, balloons, cooler and beach gear, dishpan, rice or small noodles, toy boats, pictures of the beach and ocean

AT
HOME

Your children probably enjoy reading road signs when your family is traveling. How about getting them to create signs for inside your house?

Provide sheets of poster board or shirt cardboard, on which your kids will draw signs with markers or crayons. They can also draw the signs on sheets of colored paper, then affix the paper to the cardboard with glue or tape. Suggest starting off with simple signs like STOP, which can be used where a hallway enters a busy room. Your kids can also modify real signs: NO PARKING may become NO SLEEPING when placed over the sofa. Encourage the creation of nonsense signs as well. How about WATCH FOR FALLING BANANAS or CAUTION: DINOSAUR CROSSING?

Required:

Poster board, cardboard, art supplies, double-stick tape or nontoxic glue

Maybe your family needs a SPEED LIMIT: 2 MPH sign in the hallway leading to the playroom or a NO SNACKING ZONE warning on the refrigerator. Next time your children are running inside, you can pull them over and say, "Hey, didn't you see the speed-limit sign back there?"

What better cure for cabin fever than having your child build his or her own cabin using the couch and some blankets?

For basic couch cabin construction, have your child stand the cushions on end, leaning against the front of the couch. Adding a blanket for a roof makes the rustic home ready for occupancy. If a bigger cabin for two or more kids is needed, have the troop use chairs as "poles" for hanging blankets or large towels. Also, a couple of small tables set side by side with a blanket or beach towel draped over them make a wonderful tunnel-like entrance that can lead to the "main living area."

Once the shelter is ready, details can be added to the homestead. A circle of blocks with a few sheets of crumpled red and orange paper make an ideal campfire. Larger blocks can serve as rock seats. Suggest using a floor lamp or table leg to tether a weary steed.

If the couch house is big enough for you, you might find that there are lots of advantages to living simply.

Required:

Couch, blankets or large towels, chairs, blocks, red and orange paper, pot

Optional:

Flashlight

AT
HOME

Glove Puppet

Small Parts!

Everybody loves a puppet show. Here's a way for your kids to produce one right in the kitchen. Give your child a pair of latex gloves that you don't mind sacrificing (you'll get plenty of uses out of this activity), along with some markers, tape, glue, yarn, buttons, and whatever else you have handy to transform glove fingers into a collection of puppets.

If your child wants to make a larger puppet, he or she can draw a face right on the palm of the glove. Face decorations like a mustache, eyebrows, and lips can be made from yarn. The fingers of the glove become hair.

Older kids can wear the glove, then close their hand like a fist. This makes a hand puppet where the thumb moves up and down to form a mouth. Big eyes, red lips, and a shock of yellow yarn hair are all your child needs to complete the look.

An old cereal box, with the bottom opened and the front partially cut out, can serve as a small theater. Open the paper towel curtain—it's on with the show!

Required:

Latex gloves, art supplies, yarn, cereal box, paper towel

Go Boating!

Don't have time to visit the yacht club because you have to cook dinner tonight? Then bring the club into your kitchen with a miniature "dishpan regatta."

Small Parts!

You and your kids can easily make boats and catamarans with common household items. To make a sailboat, insert a toothpick into a cork near one end (the mast). Then cut out an appropriately sized triangular sail from the plastic liner of a cereal or cracker box and tape it onto the mast. Now cut a slit into the opposite side of the cork (the bottom) and insert a dime about an eighth of an inch or deep enough so that it will stay in place. The dime will keep the boat upright in the water.

Place the boats in a dishpan filled with water, and provide your captains with straws so they can blow their craft around the water. With a bit of practice they'll be able to do fancy turns or figure eights, or maybe even set a "World Dishpan Record"!

Required:

Corks, toothpicks, plastic liner from cereal/ cracker boxes, tape, dimes, dishpan or large baking pan

AT
HOME

Here's a winning activity for sci-fi fans that involves creating a monster right in your living room. Try these production and prop tips and ideas to get started:

- Paper-bag space helmets are easy to make; tape on toilet paper tubes to create a high-tech look. The monster can wear a decorated paper-bag mask.
- Couch cushions arranged in a tunnel make great caves for beasts to emerge from.
- For low-budget special effects, pause the camera, have all the actors freeze in place, then have the monster join the scene (appearing out of thin air) before restarting the camera.
- A cityscape can be created out of empty boxes, which will collapse dramatically when the monster stomps on them.
- A paper plate covered with aluminum foil makes a great flying saucer.

Required:

Video camera, paper bags and toilet paper tubes, art supplies, cardboard boxes, newspapers, paper plate, couch cushion, table, sheet

Recommend experimenting with different story ideas: For example, a scary visitor from another planet may turn out to be a good buddy after obvious (and amusing) language difficulties are overcome and fears are put aside.

How good are your children's memories? How good is yours? Everyone will surely find out with this activity.

Have your kids imagine that everyone is at Grandma's (or any relative's) house. Then say, "I'm looking in Grandma's cupboard and I see a jar of coffee." Your child then says, "I see a jar of coffee and a jar of peanut butter." Each player repeats the list and adds another item, and the game continues until someone can't remember one of the items. Then the game starts again. You can vary the game by restricting the foods to a certain type, such as vegetables or desserts, or by deciding that foods have to be added in alphabetical order.

For the greatest challenge, players must add to the list by size, starting with the smallest item in the kitchen (maybe a spice bottle top) and progressing to the largest (probably the refrigerator).

Now, then, did anyone remember to add Grandma's pickled parsnips to the list?

Why not let your kids cast a few of their own spells while you cook. It's great fun! But first, they'll need a magic wand.

Your kids can make a wand using the cardboard tube from an old wire clothes hanger, or some other suitable thin tube. To give the tube magical properties, they can cover it with aluminum foil and tape a cardboard star to the end.

Of course, every magician needs a hat. Roll a large sheet of black construction paper into a cone. Make sure the bottom of the cone fits comfortably over your child's head. Trim the bottom so that it's even. To create an authentic look, your child can cut stars out of white paper or aluminum foil and glue them to the hat.

Required:

Art supplies, cardboard tube from wire hanger, tape

Now your little magician is all set. Just make your request, and presto! the job is done. Peel that onion without shedding a tear . . . make the laundry disappear . . . make the dishes wash themselves. Now, those are tough tricks to follow!

They're fun! They're exciting! They're "a-maz-ing!" They're super mazes, and they're sure to entertain your child while you prepare dinner.

Gather plastic spice bottles, freezer containers, cereal boxes, cans of food, and small food boxes, then arrange them into a maze. Start off by making a straight passage, then add a couple of turns. Allow several inches between the objects, and add some side tunnels. Designate a starting and an ending point.

Now see if your child can use a chopstick to maneuver a Ping-Pong ball through the maze—without touching any of the objects with his or her hands or with the chopstick. If the chopstick touches something other than the ball, the ball goes back to the starting point. Up the challenge by moving the objects closer together.

When you get a break in the cooking, stroll over to the table and see if you can master the super maze. Uh oh, maybe you ought to stick with cooking!

Required:

Common kitchen and food containers, Ping-Pong or small ball, chopstick

Required:

Paper bags

Optional:

Writing supplies, tape recorder, video camera

What happens when a group of cabin-bound kids work on a story together? Perhaps a great tale emerges.

Each child goes to a different room in the house and collects a bagful of items: a toy, a book, a shoe, a hat, and so on. (You can specify the number of items to be collected.) One child retrieves an item from his or her bag and starts off a story. Perhaps the item is a doll: "Michele decided not to go to school today because . . ." The next person pulls an item from his or her bag and adds to the tale; if the object is a shoe, the sentence might continue: ". . . her shoes were too small." This process goes on until all the items have been incorporated into the story.

As an alternative, have family members select items for one another to add to the excitement and suspense. Look around the house and imagine the wild stories that would arise using common items as props, from soup ladles to handkerchiefs!

Try to capture the story sessions on paper, tape, or video; they're sure to be a family hit.

Guess That Sound

Shhh, what's that sound? You and your child will certainly enjoy finding out. Close your eyes or turn your back and have your child find an item (either in the same room or another part of your home), then retrieve it. For younger children, you might want to preselect some unbreakable, kid-safe objects from which to choose. Your child then uses the item to make a sound, and you have to guess what the object is.

If you're stumped, ask for hints. For example, if your child is tapping the floor with your brown boots, he or she might say, "This is a sound that people sometimes make when they're walking." And if you need another clue, your child can add, "But you'd only hear this when it's snowing." Still haven't guessed it? Your child might then elaborate, "This came from your shoebox, and it matches your new jacket." Aha, you finally guessed it!

Then it's your child's turn: You choose an object and have your child guess what the sound is. For something that might sound really alien to him or her, how about the sound of running water (as in brushing teeth)?

Required:
Common household items

AT
HOME

If you have an atlas of the world, a pencil, and paper, then you have all you need to get a child or two through the "cabin fever blues." Try these geo quizzes with your geo whizzes:

- City Roster: Pick a state or country, then read off cities, starting with the most obscure and progressing to the most well known. How quickly can your kids figure out the state or country?
- Border Crossings: Choose a state or country, then see who, on the basis of bordering states or countries, can determine the place in question.
- Orientation Games (USA): List states that are north, south, east, and west of (but not bordering) the selected state, then ask who can figure out the mystery state.
- Guess-It-by-Shape: Trace a state or country and show the outline to the quiz show contenders. Can any of the players correctly identify your choice?

Required:

World atlas, paper and pencil for tracing

Encourage your kids to make up their own intriguing questions. You'll be surprised at the minutia you learn. Quick: What state is home to Ashtabula?

Guess Who

This guessing game is fun for older children, especially in a group. It's a simple "Who am I thinking of?" game, with an interesting twist in how
questions are asked and answered.

To start, have one player think of a person, either someone in the group or someone familiar to
everybody. Then, all the other participants try to
figure out who the subject is by asking questions
to get clues. The questions must all be in the form
of "If this person was a *blank,* what type of *blank*
would he or she be?" What gets filled in for
"blank" are common nouns, like *tree, car, song,* or
an article of clothing.

In answering the questions, the first player has
to try to think of some characteristic of the subject
that compares to a particular type of tree, car,
song, etc. For example, if the subject is very
strong, he or she might be described as an oak
tree. Or a tall subject could be a redwood tree.
The players should keep asking questions until
someone figures out the subject.

Now, if this person was a kid's activity, what
sort of activity would he or she be?

Here's a way to turn your hallway into a high-action sports arena. Make a "tunnel" out of empty boxes and toilet paper tubes standing on end, wide enough to accommodate a rubber ball. The goal is to roll the ball through the tunnel without knocking over any of the boxes or tubes or getting stuck.

For hotshot pinball players, decrease the tunnel width or use a larger ball that's more likely to collide with the boxes and tubes. You can also make the game more challenging by setting books in the tunnel at angles, which will deflect the course of the ball.

For added fun, your child can decorate the boxes and tubes with construction paper or crayons and markers. You can also place toys in the path; perhaps the idea of the game is to knock over the alligator or deep-sea diver at the end of the tunnel. Encourage your kids to invent their own rules, the zanier the better.

Required:

Toilet paper tubes, cardboard boxes, ball

Optional:

Crayons or markers, construction paper, books

Hat Potato

Here's a neat takeoff on "hot potato" that's fun for younger kids. To begin the game, each child needs a hat. Next, make up ten to fifteen "Hat Potato slips": small pieces of paper with simple but silly instructions written on them, such as "Hop on one foot and quack like a duck" or "Slither like a snake." Tape the slips to the outside of one of the hats (or write the instructions on stick-on notes and affix them to the designated hat). Then get a tape player ready with a selection of lively music.

Have the children sit sideways in a circle on the floor so that each child faces the back of the person's head in front of him or her. Each child also wears a hat. Once the kids are in place, turn on the music; have them remove their hats and place them on the heads of the children in front of them. This hat passing continues until you stop the music; whoever has the special hat takes one slip of paper from it and follows the directions on it (you or an older sibling can help pre-readers).

Start the music, and pass the hat for this fun circle game!

Required:
Play or real hats, writing supplies, tape player or radio

Optional:
Stick-on notes

AT
HOME

In the children's book, *Jenny's Hat*, by Ezra Jack Keats, a child is feeling bad about her plain old hat. But her bird friends come to the rescue with decorations such as a valentine, flowers, and even a bird's nest.

Even if your child doesn't have fine-feathered friends, he or she can construct a great hat. Take a strip of clear adhesive covering and wrap it around the top of your child's favorite hat, sticky side out. You might have to hold the covering paper in place with double-stick tape.

Now your child can festoon his or her hat by placing the following types of decorations on the adhesive covering: cutouts of flowers, people, animals, cars, and geometric shapes; pictures from magazines, postcards, and junk mail; cotton balls; and anything else that will make for lively headgear.

With a hat like this, your child is sure to turn some heads.

Required:

Hat, clear adhesive covering, art supplies, magazines and other picture sources, recycled materials

Would your child like to have more days off from school for national holidays? Here's his or her chance.

This antidote for the "cabin fever blues" involves inventing zany holidays for the nation or even the whole world to celebrate. To help your child brainstorm, provide a stack of newspapers, junk mail, mail order catalogs, magazines, and other photo sources. Perhaps your child is fascinated with the idea of National Fruit Juicer and Vegetable Steamer Day. Or Stamp Out Plaque Week.

Younger kids can simply talk about the holiday; older children (who can also serve as "scribes" for siblings) can create a holiday "report," complete with the picture that inspired the event, when it is supposed to take place, how long it lasts, a description of the festivities, what people are expected to wear, who should observe the event, songs to be sung, and so on.

Required:

Magazines and other picture sources, writing supplies, binder

Place the write-ups in a three-ring binder and you've got a complete holiday planner. How will *your* family be celebrating National Tree Frog Day?

Does your child have a tough time keeping all of his or her art supplies neat and accessible? Then suggest making an organizer box to sort things out.

First supply a shoebox or similar-sized carton; your child can cover it with white or craft paper, then decorate it with a personal flair. Next, have your child sort out what he or she wants to store in the box (that will determine the size and shape of the required sections).

The dividers are made from strips of thin cardboard, such as the type that dry cleaners use to package shirts. Each strip should be cut a bit longer than the space it needs to span so there's enough at the ends for your child to fold back and glue. Small cardboard gift boxes or check boxes can also be used to create divided sections. Toilet paper tubes, which make excellent paintbrush holders, can be trimmed and glued in the organizer as well. Small items like paper clips and rubber bands can be placed in envelopes that can be stored in the box.

Required:

Shoebox or carton, thin cardboard, toilet paper tubes, nontoxic glue, scissors, craft or white paper, art supplies, envelopes, small gift boxes or check boxes

When the organizer is done, your child will have a place to store all the supplies that went into making it.

Why does a piggy bank have to look like a pig? It doesn't. Here are some alternate banks you can make at home.

Mailbox Bank.   Have your kids start with an empty milk carton taped shut at the top, with a flap cut in the slanted portion. Glue half circles of cardboard at the tops of the sides, then add a third piece of cardboard curving partway over the circles to form the top. They can finish it by covering it with blue and red paper.

Frog Bank.   Supply your kids with a small box (such as a pound sugar box). Have them cover it with green construction paper. Lay the box flat. Your child can now cut out four legs from the construction paper and glue them onto the sides and front. Now, remove two compartments from an egg carton for your child to first paint green, then glue onto the top near one end of the box. Cut a slot in front of the eyes to receive coins. Your child can then use a marker to incorporate the slot into a big happy smile that says, "Feed me!"
    RRRRibbit!

Required:

Egg cartons, small boxes, milk carton, cardboard tubes, kraft or construction paper, art supplies, tape and nontoxic glue

D₀ your kids really know what's in your house? They probably think so, but these hunting challenges will get them to take a closer look.

To play, simply have your children find different items in your house that fall in certain categories or have particular characteristics. Here are a few to start with:

Color matching.   Have your kids pick something at random, then find ten items in the house that are the same color.

Double duty.   How many items can your children locate that have more than one purpose, such as a stepstool/chair?

Two by two.   Send your children through the house to find everything that comes in pairs, like shoes, bookends, socks, or closet door handles.

Majority rules.   What single item in your house outnumbers all others? The answer can be practical (light switches) or silly (pieces of yarn in your carpet).

Opposites.   Have your children find one pair of opposites (big/small, heavy/light, high/low) in every room.

On with the hunt!

How Long Before . . . ?

Most of the suspense in a kitchen centers around the age-old question: "When's dinner?" Here's a neat way to inject a little anticipation into cooking time, good for one child or a group of hungry kitchen kids.

To play, your child picks a kitchen object (the spatula, the slotted spoon, or the small saucepan, for example). Then, he or she tracks how much time passes before you use it. Or, if your kitchen has tile floors, your child can choose a particular tile and then see how long it is before you step on it.

If more than one child is playing, each one chooses an object. The winner can either be the person who correctly picks the first or last object actually used.

With this activity, your cooking will get more attention than you ever imagined possible. And your kids will be glued to the edge of their seats!

This activity can help take the edge off cabin fever whenever your children feel the need to "get their sillies out."

On three-by-five-inch index cards, write various antics that your kids can perform. Organize the actions by categories, such as Animal Impersonations ("Roar like a lion") or Acts of Dexterity ("Hold a ball in your open hand and hop around the room two times").

Have your kids decorate the backs of the cards with crayons or markers. Encourage them to keep the categories consistent so that all blue cards will be Animal Impersonations, all red cards will be Acts of Dexterity, and so on.

Required:

Pencil and index cards, large sheet of paper, art supplies, socks

Next, place a large piece of paper on the floor. Use crayons or markers to draw a "target." Color in each ring of the target, making sure all of the colors of your cards are represented on the target. Place the cards near the throwing line, organized in color-matched stacks. Each player tosses a rolled-up pair of socks onto the target, picks a card the same color as the circle that his or her sock landed in, then follows the instructions.

Sound silly? Then you've got it!

Wouldn't you like to hear what you thought and did when you were young, in your own words and your own voice? Well, you can't go back in time, but you can help your child record his or her feelings and experiences on tape and create a treasure that will be appreciated for many years.

To begin, have your child tell you about some important events in his or her life in the past week or month. Encourage him or her to include anything at all that comes to mind (your child may find it helpful if you go first by telling something about what you've been doing). Some topics to include are school experiences, activities with friends, visits with relatives, or family outings. Once your child is ready, set up a tape recorder with a blank tape so he or she can begin recording a diary on tape.

Required:
tape recorder

Who knows, these tapes may end up as part of a documentary when your child grows up to be a famous person.

Everybody loves a cookout. Here's how your kids can have their own without fire or charcoal.

To make a barbecue, your child fills a dishpan with building blocks, crumpled black construction paper, or newspaper (charcoal). A wire cooling rack, placed over the dishpan, makes a grill. Then set the barbecue on four wooden blocks (legs). Red and yellow blocks can stand in for fire.

Of course, your barbecue chef will need special cookout equipment: tongs, oven mitts, and an apron. Your child can make skewers out of straws (perfect for grilling marshmallows and shish kebab). Turkey basters will also come in handy for marinating the meal.

Required:

Dish pan, wire cooling rack, wooden blocks, art supplies, cookout equipment

Finally, your child can use his or her imagination to make foods and store them in the grill for the next time he or she wants to play.

One thing is certain: This cookout will never get rained out!

Indoor Olympics

The Olympics, the pinnacle of sports achievement, right in your living room! You can stage your own indoor Olympics by putting together an assortment of simple sports challenges for your kids. To get your children into the spirit of the games, have them put together their own Olympic uniforms (T-shirts, pj's, sweats, etc.) and start off with these indoor sporting events:

Adult Supervision

Slither race. Contestants slither along the length of the room on their stomachs, without using their arms or hands.

Balance beam. Athletes walk on a piece of string on the floor.

Weight lifting. Tie two onion-bag balls (activity 143) to a wrapping paper tube for a pretend weight-lifting competition.

Suggested:

String, onion bag balls (see activity 143), wrapping paper tube

Triathlon. Combine three simple activities for a triathlon event.

Knee races. Have the competitors kneel on the rug for this race.

Signal the start of the games with a shout from a toilet paper kazoo and watch the athletes strut their stuff!

AT
HOME

Even Sherlock Holmes had to start somewhere en route to becoming a great detective. Here's how to get your child started on the road to finding clues that lead to great treasures.

As in the traditional treasure hunt, the idea is to place clues around the house, with the first clue leading your child to the second, the second to the third, and so on, until he or she reaches the treasure (a cookie or appropriate treat, perhaps).

The twist here is to rename the rooms of the house and devise appropriate clues. For instance, the kitchen might be named the North Pole, and a clue leading to the refrigerator might read, "Find the paper stuck to the giant iceberg of the North Pole." Younger children can join in the fun by having older kids read and interpret the clues.

Play this a sufficient number of times and you might just launch your child's professional detective career.

Required:

Writing supplies

Optional:

Cookie or treat

In-Print Hunt

Here's a "find it" game that will keep your pre-readers poring through books, magazines, and newspapers in search of items that you specify for them to locate. Use these categories for starters:

Things That Move. Have them look for pictures of trains, boats, cars, trucks, airplanes, bicycles, skates, and so on.

Animals. Keep the animal picture hunt simple for younger kids by having them find big animals and small animals.

Colors. First have your children point to, say, all the green things, followed by all the red things, etc.

Different Parts of the House. How many pictures of kitchens, bedrooms, bathrooms, and the like can your kids find?

Required:

Books, magazines, and other print sources

Shapes. See how many round things your children can find, then square things, and so on.

Finally, how about locating happy faces, which we hope you'll see when your kids do this activity!

Here's how you can help your child understand that any age is a great age to be.

Give your child three or four sheets of paper, a pencil, and verbal instructions to write his or her current age at the top of the first page. On subsequent pages, your child can write some of the important ages he or she has been (a ten-year-old might have pages entitled "ten," "six," "two," and "newborn").

Then ask your child to make a list of all the best things about being each of those ages. He or she can include abilities, privileges, events, hopes and ambitions, and so on. For example, on the "newborn" page, your child might list: "Met my family," "Learned new things all the time," etc. Under "two," he or she might write: "Learned to run," "Made my first friends," "Visited Grandma," and so on.

Required:
Writing supplies, stapler

When your child is finished writing, staple the pages together and put them in a safe place. He or she can add to it periodically upon discovering the best things about being an older kid.

Junior Appliances

Every junior cook needs some countertop appliances to get the evening meal on the table on time.

Small Parts!

How about a blender or food processor? It's certainly one of the more useful gadgets in the kitchen, and your child can easily make one from a cylindrical oatmeal container. After pasting a piece of white paper around the container, he or she can draw horizontal lines indicating different measurements. A small box, covered with paper, can serve as the base. Affix a jar cap as a speed control knob.

Or how about a toaster—it's not just for breakfast! Have your kids draw a couple of long, thin rectangles in the top of a box for you to cut out. Then, cut some "bread" from paper plates.

Next time one of your own appliances is on the blink, perhaps your kids will be kind enough to lend you theirs!

Required:
Oatmeal container, small boxes, art supplies, bottle and jar caps

Even if you don't have Chinese food tonight, you can enjoy fortune cookies. Have your child write out custom fortunes for each member of the family and place them in envelopes, empty film canisters, or other small containers. Your child can also help you set the table and place loose fortunes under family members' placemats or plates. The fortunes might focus on topics such as:

Upcoming events. "You will ace your history test."

Household events. "It will be sunny for our picnic on Sunday."

Required:
Writing supplies, envelopes, film canisters and other containers

Fanciful thinking. "A great tornado will straighten up your room tomorrow."

Hopeful thinking. "Mom will bake your favorite cookies today."

Very hopeful thinking. "Dad will lose his new low-fat, low-salt, no-sugar cookbook."

So, what does the soothsayer believe your prospects are for getting through the day without an attack of cabin fever?

If your child is handy with tools, perhaps he or she would like to open up a hardware store right at home.

Have your child gather the inventory and arrange the items by category: paper towel tubes and toy rings (for the hardware department), cardboard and poster board (for lumber), straws and milk jugs (for the plumbing area), and so on.

Then, become your child's first customer. Walk into the store, describe a mechanical "problem" that you're having around the house, and see whether your child has the gadget and the know-how to solve it.

And while you're at it, you might want to have your child duplicate some keys, repair a broken appliance, or explain how to begin a home improvement project (and sell you the supplies you'll need to complete it).

Maybe a combination wall-smoother/floor-leveler is just what you need to refinish your basement . . .

Required:

Paper towel tubes, cardboard and poster board, straws, milk jugs, toy rings

A soft foam or rubber ball is just the thing to get a few kitchen games off and rolling, and entertain you and your kids while you cook.

Have your kids set up ten paper cups (preferably recycled) on the floor. Mark a line with a piece of masking tape, or designate a certain line between floor tiles. Your kids stand behind the line and roll the ball at the cups. Older kids can keep score.

With a few modifications, the bowling alley becomes a giant arcade game—simply arrange the cups into an alley, with one or two slightly extending into the path. The goal is to try to roll the ball through the alley without touching a cup.

And when your kids are done with the bowling and arcade games, suggest a little putting practice to build up a good appetite. Set a plastic pitcher on its side on the floor and provide a wrapping paper tube. Your kids can take turns using the tube as a putter and the pitcher as the hole.

Required:

Foam or soft rubber ball, paper cups, plastic pitcher, wrapping paper tube

Kitchen Musicians

Want some sweet music to accompany you while you cook? Our old babysitter, Betsy, told us to look no further than our recycling bin . . . and our young musicians. Here's her recommendation:

Take three one-liter plastic soda bottles and tape them together in a triangle. Then have your child put a small amount of water in one bottle (about half an inch), two inches in the next, and four inches in the next. Your child then blows over (and slightly into) the bottles. The bottle with the smaller amount of water will make a lower tone than those that contain more water.

Your child can experiment with different amounts of water, or with different configurations of bottles. Groups of kids can each make their own soda bottle instruments, then coordinate on a song or two.

And when the orchestra is done for the day, the members simply toss their instruments into the recycling bin. Bet the New York Philharmonic doesn't have it so easy!

Required:

Empty one-liter plastic soda bottles, tape

AT
HOME

It may be a long way until dinner, but your kids can stay occupied with this leisure-time favorite—an indoor version of shuffleboard.

All your kids need to play is a set of lids from some old butter tubs or plastic storage containers. Divide the "pucks" and set up scoring on squares of kitchen tiles. One tile might be worth 1, another 3, and another 5. Players scoot a puck across the floor toward the *scoring* tiles by tossing it Frisbee-style or flicking it with their fingers.

Players score if their pucks land perfectly within a square. If a puck is over the line, it doesn't count. Also, it's legal for one player to knock another player's puck out of a scoring position.

Required:

Plastic lids

Your kids can keep score for a set number of rounds, play to a predetermined number, or play "sudden death," in which a winner is declared after each round. This works well right before mealtime, as the rounds can be finished up quickly.

And then everyone can shuffle off to the table to eat!

Label Master

Have you ever read a food label? All you get is the percentage of fat and vitamins. The really good *information*, like the percentage of yummi-ness, is nowhere to be found.

Your kids can remedy that situation—and stay busy while you work—by creating their own food labels for all sorts of packaged foods in your kitchen. All they need are a few colored markers or crayons, paper, and transparent tape.

Even kids too young to write can join in the fun by decorating labels with pictures. Kids who have writing skills can invent their own ingredi-ents that go into the cereal, the soup, and the crackers (high in cement and tree bark, and a great source of Vitamin X23).

Required:
Art supplies

Have your kids affix the labels to the food packages with tape—the next time someone goes into the pantry for a snack, they might be relieved to learn that their favorite chips *are* 100 percent lightning and snow-free!

AT
HOME

Your kids don't need a license or a pond to play this fun fishing game, which is especially suited to young children.

Have your child gather some of his or her small toys. Drop the toys into a large plastic container. You can use a storage bowl, a dish pan, or any other suitable container.

Next, give your child a ladle to use as a "fishing pole." The idea is to catch the object that you ask for: "the small yellow block" or "the little green alligator."

If your child "reels" in the wrong toy, he or she has to toss it back. As you get breaks during your dinner preparations, comment on the game with phrases like "Oh, looks like that blue bear got away from you there," or "The Legos don't seem to be biting today."

Required:

Large plastic container, ladle, small toys

When supper's on the table, your little one can regale the family with his or her own fish stories. "And you should have seen the one that got away . . ."

Lid Games

This fast-moving lid game will keep things flying in the kitchen—including the time!

To start a round of lid games, have your kids gather a selection of plastic bowls, margarine tubs, and other storage containers with lids. Remove all the lids, then see how quickly your kids can get all the lids back on the right containers. One player will need to keep an eye on the time (or you can do that if you have a break in your cooking).

As a variation, your kids can set the kitchen timer and try to beat the clock when putting the lids back on. With each round they give themselves less and less time, and the excitement builds as the kids try to get all of the lids on before the timer goes off.

Finally, your kids can play the game with a blindfold. Shuffle the lids, then blindfold the first player. That player, with a little verbal coaching, must put the lids on the correct containers.

After a few rounds of these games, your kids will be able to organize all your containers—with their eyes closed!

Required:

Plastic tubs with lids, blindfold, kitchen timer

Even when you're cabin-bound, the world outside is constantly changing. Here's an activity your child can begin in the morning, continue at intervals (say, every hour) throughout the day, and finish at dinnertime. Have him or her look out the window (the same window each time) and write a paragraph or draw a picture about what he or she sees *at that moment*. Emphasize changing or moving items (clouds, cars and trucks, pets, etc.). During each "window-watching" session, your child can update his or her notes or draw a new picture.

You can have your own "parallel" window-watching sessions. Accompany your child to the window every hour or so and write descriptions or draw "photos" of what *you* see. At the end of the day (or activity), compare *your* vision of what's out the window with your child's. Discuss the changes each of you saw. Not only is it likely you noticed some different things, but it's also possible that you and your child have entirely separate views of the very same neighborhood.

Required:

Pencil and paper and/or art supplies

Macaroni Math

Let's see, how does that old song go? "Stuck a feather in his cap and called it vermicelli." We may be confused about "Yankee Doodle," but your kids won't be mixed up about addition or subtraction when they use macaroni noodles to do some math.

Small Parts!

Give your child some noodles (for very young children, keep the number of macaroni noodles under ten) and a placemat or dish. Then, as you're cooking, present your child with simple arithmetic problems. You might, for example, say: "How much is two plus four?" To find the answer, your child counts out the appropriate number of noodles and tells you what the total is.

Older children who can handle larger numbers can use different-colored noodles to calculate higher totals. Each color can represent a different amount: Yellows are ones, reds are tens, greens are hundreds. Your child can line up the noodles in columns and add or subtract the appropriate amounts.

Required:

Macaroni noodles

Entertaining your kids while you cook isn't so hard. You just have to make every minute count!

As this activity will prove, imagination is the real mother of invention.

Gather up an assortment of art supplies, odds and ends, lids, spools, foil, and shoeboxes and have your child build an imaginary machine (one that turns spinach into ice cream, sounds an alarm when baby brother enters the room, or polishes the cat's claws). Your child can start with a plain shoebox and add plastic lids and paper arrows for dials, cardboard tubes for feeding in "raw material," and yarn for "drive belts." Encourage the inventor to decide on a purpose for every piece he or she puts on the machine. Suggest decorating the devices with tempera paint, markers, recycled foil, and pictures cut out of magazines, junk mail, catalogs, and so on.

Later, say after dinner, have your child make a presentation to the rest of the family, explaining in detail what the gadget does and how it works. (This will be great to catch on videotape, if you can.)

Just one question: Does the cat get to pick which color claw polish she wants?

Required:

Boxes, recycled household materials, magazines and other photo sources, art supplies, tape and nontoxic glue

Optional:

Video camera

Make an Ad

Are you and your child tired of seeing the same old newspaper and magazine ads? Here's how to take revenge on the advertising pros.

Browse through newspapers and magazines, then clip photos as well as bits and pieces of copy from ads, reassembling them into wacky hybrids that parody or spoof the originals. Add a wild headline (the more incongruous the better), then affix all the pieces with glue or double-stick tape to a sheet of paper or poster board.

When you and your child have finished your "ad campaigns," pass the ads back and forth or take turns reading the headlines and text aloud, seeing who can suppress their giggles the longest. If a group is playing, each participant can stand up and do a dramatic reading of his or her ad.

Twenty percent off the price of ear polish that three out of four city senators recommend? Sounds great to us . . .

Required:

Magazines, newspapers, and other photo and text sources; double-stick tape or nontoxic glue; paper or poster board; scissors

AT
HOME

Who's cooking at your house? Your kids with their own stove, that's who.

Take an empty large carton, tape both ends closed, and make a door by drawing a square on the front of the box, then cutting the square on three sides so that it swings open (your job).

Next, your kids can trace circles above the door using the narrow end of small paper cups. Cut out the circles. Your kids then insert the bottoms of the cups through the holes from inside the box—presto, instant dials. Your kids can draw designs on the dials to match those on your stove or oven.

Required:

Large carton, paper cups, paper plates, tape, art supplies

Your kids can also easily make burners on the top of the stove by tracing circles around different-sized pan lids. Or they may want to glue paper plates on top of the box—that is, stove.

Your kids are really cooking now!

If your child is fascinated by maps, this activity will beat a path to fun and learning.

Start with an area most familiar to your child: the backyard or the area surrounding your house or apartment. Suggest that he or she draw landmarks such as a garage, steps, a fence, garden, sandbox, and so on. Also suggest drawing the compass directions, but don't worry about the accuracy of the map; the idea is simply to allow your child to express his or her understanding of local geography.

Once the backyard is drawn, expand the map or start a new sheet so that it covers a block or two and includes the streets and their names, the houses of neighbors and friends, stores, traffic lights, stop signs, and any noteworthy landscape features your child can recall.

Required:
Writing supplies, art supplies

Then see if he or she can chart the entire town in which you live, perhaps even expanding to the state and including various cities. Again, don't fret about accuracy; this mapping activity is measured in units of F-U-N.

Adult Supervision

Here's a new twist (or more accurately, shake, rattle, and roll) on painting that your child is sure to enjoy.

Provide a large box, then have your child place a piece of paper inside. If the box is significantly larger than the paper, tape down the edges with masking tape. Next, give your child a handful of marbles (supervise carefully if young children will be participating in the activity; Ping-Pong balls may be more appropriate). Your child covers the marbles with tempera paint, then places them on the paper in the box. As he or she shakes the box, the marbles will create interesting swirls and patterns.

Required:

Cardboard box, marbles or Ping-Pong balls, tempera paint, paper, masking tape

Encourage experimentation: Perhaps your child might introduce one marble at a time or place the marbles in the four corners of the box before beginning the shaking action.

As your child gets more comfortable controlling the roll of the marbles, he or she can try to create specific patterns. For the ultimate challenge, see if your child can write his or her name in "marblelese."

Marshmallow on the Moon

What has no feathers and flies? Why, a marshmallow, launched from a spoon!

To find out for yourself, provide each of your kids with a plastic or metal spoon. The handle must be flat, so that a marshmallow can rest on it while your child slaps the round part, catapulting the marshmallow into the air.

Place the spoons behind a "launching line" (a string, a chopstick, etc.) on the floor or table. Then arrange a series of targets, such as container tops or paper plates. Your kids can write numbers or words on pieces of paper and affix them to the targets, or write directly on the targets with markers.

Place the targets a couple of feet away from the spoon launchers, and let the games begin!

Players take turns slapping the spoons and trying to plunk their marshmallows onto the desired targets. Perhaps when there's a lull in the cooking, you can try it, too. Nice shot, but we wonder how your marinara sauce will taste with that marshmallow floating in it!

Required:

Spoons, large marshmallows, plastic lids or paper plates, markers

AT
HOME

This game is a combination of Follow-the-Leader and Concentration that will make paying attention fun for a group of cabin-bound kids.

Gather the players in a spot with a good view of one or more rooms in the house, pick a person to start, and have everyone watch carefully as he or she walks to an object and touches it before returning to the group. Then, have the next player repeat the actions of the first child and add a second item to the selection by touching it. Each child in turn repeats the steps of the previous one and adds something else.

You can challenge the group to try to remember, say, ten items or have the players limit their selections to particular types of objects, such as things you sit on. You can also have them do something more complicated than just touching an item; they could, for instance, pick up a book or magazine and read one sentence out of it.

Uh-oh, it's your turn, the magazine just blew shut, you can't remember which plant Sam touched, and the cat is leaving the room.

Money in the Bank

Who needs automatic teller machines when you can have a bank right at home and set your own hours?

Adult Supervision

Have your child set up a "teller's window" with deposit and withdrawal slips (cut-up junk mail or pieces of used paper), a pen on a chain (or string), a computer terminal (made from boxes), and a cash register (an egg carton). Supply some coins, too (supervise closely if toddlers will be joining the play).

See whether your younger child can help you with some simple transactions (like accepting money for a deposit or cashing a check). Your older child might assist you with more complicated banking matters (counting change, exchanging your money for foreign currency, issuing traveler's checks, and so on).

Required:

Cardboard boxes, egg carton, writing supplies, chain or string, junk mail

Then, trade places. You become the teller and your child can take on the role of the customer. Your child might just learn a valuable lesson while he or she is banking: Money really doesn't grow in egg cartons.

A young person with lots of great ideas for fun, Sarah Provo, told us that a terrific way to entertain yourself is to describe the world to an imaginary friend. Here's a kitchen-time adaptation.

Ask your child to imagine that a friend from another time or planet has come to visit, and is quite baffled by all of the gadgets and appliances in your kitchen. Your child's job is to explain each item—what it does and how it works. You play the part of the onlooker, prompting your child to explain things that both of you take for granted.

For example, you might point to the can opener and ask your child to explain what it is. After your child identifies it, see if he or she can describe how the gear mechanism works. Or the refrigerator—just what makes it cold? And that funny box on the counter (the microwave)— what's the magic behind it?

When you finish this game you'll probably have answers to those big questions you've been wondering about all these years—like how the telephone knows it's time to ring right when you sit down to dinner.

Muffin Tin Toss

Small Parts!

When you break out the muffin tins for this game, your kids will probably expect something special for dessert. But this is a quick game to keep them happy *before* mealtime.

Kids set the muffin tins on the floor and assign points for each cup. The players take turns tossing an object into the tins, such as beans, dried macaroni, or pennies. (Small objects aren't appropriate for small kids.) If your kids are old enough to use coin math in the game, they can make "heads" worth a single score, while "tails" is worth double the amount.

As a variation, the players can toss with their eyes closed. They can also write a number on scraps of colored paper, one for each cup in the tin. Numbers on the green scraps might be positive, while those on the red scraps are to be subtracted from the score.

Required:
Muffin tins, small household objects

Optional:
Colored paper and writing supplies

AT
HOME

Can you and your child co-author a great story knowing only a minimum of what the other is plotting? Find out with this activity.

Set up a workspace (if possible, choose a room with a door) and arrange a tape recorder on the table. Have your child leave the room, then record the title and the first couple of lines of your story. When you reach a "cliffhanger" (an exciting spot in the narrative or simply the word "and"), hit the stop button and ask your child to come back into the room. Tell him or her the last five words of your recording, then leave the room. Your child then records a couple of lines to the story and tells you his or her last five words as you switch roles. Continue in this fashion until the story reaches a conclusion.

Required:

Tape recorder

When the narrative is complete, play back the tape with the two of you in the room. You're bound to get a few chuckles as the tale takes some strange twists and turns.

What's the connection between an avocado and an aardvark? Find out with this activity!

Hold up whatever ingredient you're using and say its name. You and your child have to come up with as many words as you can that start with the same letter as the object (they don't necessarily have to be food-related).

For example, hold up an egg. Immediately, the words start: "elephant," "elf," "extraterrestrial" . . . To give yourselves some variety, try thinking of words that begin with the last letter of the food, or words that rhyme with the food.

A more sophisticated version, for older kids, involves thinking of opposites. If the item in the recipe is round, kids have to think of a square food (box of cereal or brick of cheese). If it's soft, then the goal is to come up with something hard. Same with qualities like "bitter" and "sweet," and so on.

Now, then, what's the opposite of broccoli?

Napkins add class to any family meal. They're also helpful when you're wiping oatmeal off the baby's face.

While you're busy cooking, your child can make up a snazzy napkin holder for the family table; with a bit of work, the holder should be ready to grace the table for the dinner meal.

Provide a small, youth-sized shoebox that your child can cover with white paper, then decorate with markers or crayons. The decorations might be thematic with your kitchen (incorporating various colors and patterns), cooking-oriented (featuring tracings or drawings of kitchen tools), or simply abstract patterns created freehand.

Required:

Art supplies, shoebox, napkins

Place the napkins in the shoebox, and put the box at the center of the table so everyone can enjoy it. The shoebox also makes a great place to store napkin rings (see activity 107).

Now, if your kids could just fashion a drip-proof bib for the baby!

Neat Napkin Rings

Imagine the ambiance of your kitchen if everyone had his or her own personalized, handcrafted napkin ring. Well, imagine no more—with a few cardboard tubes and some art supplies, your napkins will be the talk of the kitchen!

Before you start cooking, slice toilet paper or paper towel tubes into one-and-a-half-inch sections (your job). Then cut out one-and-a-half-inch strips of paper. Your child can decorate the strips and affix them to the outside of the tube sections with glue or double-stick tape. A layer of clear adhesive wrap will protect the paper from spills.

Your kids can decorate the napkin rings with people's initials, names, favorite animals, and so on, using crayons, markers, and other art supplies. Perhaps some mini-scenes will brighten up the day—a beach scene might be just the pick-me-up for family members on a snowy day.

Alternatively, kids with writing abilities can create "fortune" napkin rings that offer cheery predictions. How about this one: "Your taste buds will be dancing tonight!"

Required:

Paper tubes, art supplies, nontoxic glue or double-stick tape, clear adhesive wrap

You're tuned to radio station WBZR, where the weather is always bizarre and the news is always unbelievable. Have your child use a tape recorder to create nutty news, silly sportscasts, and wacky weather reports. To get your child's imagination rolling, read these samples:

"Smallville was rocked today by the news that Miller's Pond is being overrun by giant blue catfish. The local game warden has come up with a plan to introduce even bigger orange dogfish to control the situation. No word yet on availability of giant dogcatcher fish in any color."

"At the World Standing-on-One-Foot Championships today there was an upset when Michael Smith lost his balance after only ten minutes. Jennifer Long was disqualified early on in the competition due to illegal nose-twitching."

Required:

Tape recorder

Encourage your child to embellish his or her radio personalities with silly voices and funny names. "Reporting for WBZR, this is Billy Banana. Now back to Sarah Spaghetti in the newsroom."

What *really* happens while the family sleeps? Ask your child to "publish" a book about his or her nighttime visions.

Your child can write a fanciful story about all the things that the household furniture and appliances do while he or she is asleep (for instance, the table might stretch its legs, the teakettle might whistle show tunes, and the telephone might call a friend). Your child might also incorporate other nonhuman characters, such as those gremlins who hide things when we're not looking.

Alternatively, your child might want to take a more serious tack and write about some of the things that actually happen while he or she sleeps (such as adults staying up late to finish household chores, nocturnal animals foraging for food, and people in other parts of the world getting ready to start the day).

This book, when finished, will undoubtedly make a very interesting bedtime story.

Required:

Writing supplies, stapler, binder or report cover

AT
HOME

Do your kids like puzzles? One of the favorite diversions around our house is solving mazes. Your child can build his or her own, right in the kitchen.

This activity is perfect if you're making spaghetti, because your kids will use cooked spaghetti noodles to make their maze. Your child takes the noodles and arranges them so that there's one path from beginning to end, cutting them as needed. If your puzzle-maker wants to get fancy, he or she can create the mazes on a paper plate—a circular maze is sure to pose some interesting problems.

When the maze is ready, take a break from your cooking, set the timer, and see if you can find your way from beginning to end before the buzzer goes off, running a chopstick along the noodle pathways.

This might be the only puzzle in your house that, after solving it, you can douse with a little sauce and eat!

Required:

Art supplies, cooked spaghetti noodles

Optional:

Paper plates

Small Parts!

The noodle is the artist's best friend, as our son, Noah, once pointed out to us while we boiled a pot of ziti. Here's how to prove it.

Provide an assortment of uncooked small noodles, such as ziti, corkscrew, radiatore, rigatoni, and penne. Your child presses one end onto a washable stamp pad, or dips it in a thin layer of tempera paint, then presses the inked or painted end onto a piece of paper to create scenes, people, abstract art, or even write messages in "noodlese."

Another way to do noodle painting is to make a "brush" ahead of time by gluing noodles of varying lengths across two Popsicle sticks (like a segment of picket fence, with the Popsicle sticks serving as rails and the noodles as pickets). Before the glue sets, press a piece of cardboard along the bottoms of the noodles so they're flush. Let the noodles dry, then glue two Popsicle sticks perpendicular to the "fence rails"; this is the handle. When that's dried, dip the "brush" into tempera paint and get set for some exciting art.

Hey, Noah, THAT's using your noodle!

Required:
Uncooked noodles, washable ink pad or tempera paint, four Popsicle sticks, nontoxic glue, paper

AT
HOME

Want to hear a great story? Then create one with your child, a word at a time. (As you'll see, this is also a neat activity to do with a word processor.)

Have your child say or write any word to begin the tale. Then you add a word, and your child adds another, until the first sentence is finished. This cooperative writing approach continues until the story comes to a conclusion. It may or may not be the ending you had envisioned, but that's the whole point: You never know what direction the tale will take when you and your child become co-authors.

Once you've gotten the hang of co-writing a story in this fashion, up the ante by introducing a new rule: No one can use the words "or," "and," or "but." That's a lot more difficult than it sounds. Take turns inventing new rules, too, just to keep each other on your toes.

Gee, that's going to be tough when you can only use words less than five letters long . . .

Required:
Writing Supplies

Optional:
Word processor

Number Hunt

Do you notice the numbers you see throughout the day, especially in your own kitchen? Chances are, your kids usually don't. Here's a simple game that opens their eyes and gives them a start on basic number skills.

The object of the game is to find all of the numbers that are visible in the kitchen; everything's fair game. The clock and measuring cups are obvious. Cereal box labels and the like are subtler.

If several children play, they can work together as a team, trying to create the highest value by adding up numbers from one object. (Hint: Many packaged foods have a customer service telephone number somewhere on the label—that will bring up the totals.) For an added challenge, suggest that players must find numbers in consecutive order.

So, what's the biggest number in your kitchen today?

Small Parts!

This activity involves building a do-it-yourself arcade toss. And it gives you a reputation as the kitchen funmeister.

Provide a large sheet of paper, then have your kids search the kitchen for round objects of different sizes, such as pot lids and soup bowls. The arcade designers trace the rims with crayons to create concentric circles on the paper. After they finish their tracings, they can color in the rings, creating a target that will be placed on the floor.

Next, make a few bean bags by dropping a handful of beans inside plastic sandwich bags and sealing them with twist ties. Place each bag inside a sock, and close with another twist tie.

The game begins as your kids take turns tossing the bags at the target. Younger children can keep score by seeing if their bags can land on each color at least once. Older kids can assign points to each target ring and try for high or low scores.

Maybe when the cumulative score reaches 100 points, it will be time for dinner!

Required:
Sheet of paper, crayons, round kitchen objects, dry beans, twist ties, sandwich bags, socks

Does your playroom or child's bedroom look as though a tornado hit it? Here's how to find some emergency relief and prevent future disasters.

Gather cardboard boxes of various shapes and sizes. Have your child cover them with craft paper (lids should be covered separately). Decorations can include photographs from magazines and junk mail catalogues (perhaps you can even find and use photos of the toys themselves) or free-hand crayon or paint designs.

Have your child decide which box will contain which type of toy (perhaps the largest box will contain giant stuffed animals, medium-sized boxes will hold building blocks or large dinosaurs, and the smallest boxes will hold Legos, marbles, etc.). Have your child label each box with its contents and his or her name.

Then make a game of having your child put the toys into their new places: For example, challenge your child to fill a box in five minutes or do the two-foot toy toss, which entails tossing soft toys into their bins from two feet away. Quick, put the lids on before the toys can escape!

Required:

Cardboard boxes, craft paper, art supplies, magazines and other photo sources

AT
HOME

Why settle for conventionally sized checkers when your kids can create a giant checker set that's as fun to make as it is to play with?

To start, gather twenty-four paper plates or plastic lids and have your children decorate them so that they have two sets of twelve "checkers" each. (If you use plastic lids, you'll probably need to glue on circles of paper to make decorating easier.) Have the kids decorate the bottoms of the playing pieces with a distinctive design (like a crown or a royal face) so that a piece can be flipped over to show that it is a "king."

Next, have your children cut sixty-four squares of paper (thirty-two each of two colors) slightly larger than the playing pieces; you might need to draw cutting lines for them. They should then place the squares on the floor in an eight-by-eight square grid with colors alternating and tape the edges together as they go.

Now clear your room; you're dealing with major-league games!

Required:

Paper plates or plastic lids, regular tape, double-stick tape or nontoxic glue, art supplies

A helmet can be the defining part of a dress-up or role-playing costume. Here's how your child can make quick and imaginative ones from paper bags.

To begin, gather up a variety of paper bags, as well as markers, scissors, scraps of cloth and paper, cardboard tubes, and other decorative add-ons. Prepare each bag for your child to decorate by folding the top down three or four times to form a one-inch rim. Then cut out part of the bag to expose some or all of your child's facial features: You can make eye or nose holes, a single "viewing band," or an opening for the entire face.

When the cutting is done, have your child use markers to transform it into a particular type of helmet (football, space, motorcycle, whatever). Suggest gluing cardboard tubes on the sides for lights or space thrusters and making similar use of other recycled materials. Your child can even cover the helmet with scraps of fabric to turn it into a bird headdress.

If your child uses his or her noggin, there's no limit to the kinds of helmets that will come out of your headgear factory.

Required:

Paper bags, art supplies, recycled materials

"What's for dinner?" Do you get that twenty or thirty times during your cooking? Go ahead and tell—then let your child turn your answer into an art project.

Sitting at a table covered with paper, your child asks questions about what you're cooking. As you answer, his or her task is to draw the finished meal. For example, your child might draw a delicious roasted chicken with heat rising from two plump drumsticks. He or she might also sketch in glasses of milk and bowls of cut vegetables surrounding the bird, as well as mashed potatoes, salads, or whatever else is on tonight's menu.

Required:

Paper or bags for covering table, art supplies

On the zanier side, your kids can take a cue from *Gulliver's Travels* and include small characters in their illustrations. Perhaps there are mountain climbers scaling the sides of that chicken. Maybe there's a high dive over the mashed potatoes! Your kids might even try to illustrate the whole family at dinner.

Say, is that dad swimming in the gravy boat?

Party-Blower Target Shoot

We've all played with noisemakers that unfurl a paper tube when you blow through them. Here's how to use them in a new way.

Gather up some lightweight targets and one party blower for each player. Toilet paper tubes, dominoes, and empty single-serving raisin boxes all make great targets.

For a warm-up game, line up five to ten targets on a table and have each player knock them over one at a time with the party blower.

Now try randomly arranging numbered targets on the table and see if your children can knock them down in order. Or place a row of targets down the middle of a table and have two players try to knock them down from opposite sides.

Yet another variation is to have your children play "party-blower hockey" using a Ping-Pong ball for a puck, with opposing teams trying to score goals by knocking the ball off the opponents' side of the table. One nice feature of this game: Every goal automatically includes a noisemaker celebration!

Required:

Party noisemakers, toilet paper tubes, dominoes, small boxes

What would a party of three (or four or five) find intriguing about your kitchen or dining room "restaurant"? Find out with this kooky activity.

The idea is for your child to develop a unique identity for your in-home restaurant. Perhaps it's an animal theme, say the Teddy Bear Bistro. Your child could place stuffed animals, along with picture books of bears, around the room.

Your child can also play the part of the maître d' and dress up for the occasion. For the Circus Cafe, he or she might don a clown suit (perhaps a Halloween leftover).

Finally, if you have a tape recorder handy, your child might want to include some special music or sound effects. For the Circus Cafe, your child could create a selection of pipe organ imitations, interspersed with authentic animal sounds, ringmaster announcements, and a round of enthusiastic applause. Your patrons just might expect to see a tiger walk through the door any minute!

Required:
Stuffed animals and other toys

Optional:
Costumes, tape recorder

Pasta Finery and More

Uncooked noodles are perfect for making necklaces and artistic creations. Here are some starter suggestions.

Small Parts!

Your child can simply string small noodles to make the necklace, or he or she can make a more elaborate creation by decorating the noodles with paint or markers, or gluing on glitter or sequins. For variety, your child might add other food items like Cheerios, half-inch lengths of straws, or plastic caps with holes (punched by you).

In addition to making necklaces, your child can make pasta wall hangings that will liven up any kitchen. Tie eight to ten two-foot-long pieces of string to a long-handled wooden spoon or a chopstick, and have your child thread the strings through noodles and other items. The end of the string should be tied to the last item.

Required:

Tubular pasta, string, Cheerios, straws, caps, art supplies, chopstick or long-handled spoon

When your child is done making the finery or wall hanging, display the artwork prominently for all family members to see after dinner. Perhaps your child will even let older siblings or you or your spouse wear the finery to school or work!

Here's a neat way to keep your child entertained—and stimulate his or her creativity during busy cooking sessions.

The idea is for your child to draw a person using different kinds of food for various body parts. A head of lettuce, for instance, could become a person's head. Carrot or celery sticks could become legs, and radish slices could serve as eyes. Your child can even make up stories that go along with his or her food people.

As an alternative to drawing, kids can cut pictures of food out of magazines and newspapers, then arrange and glue them into people shapes. They can also arrange them into animals—a can of dog food standing on four dog biscuits would make for an interesting canine creature.

Provide enough circulars and your kids will have a whole town's worth of food people out walking their food dogs and cats!

Required:
Art supplies

Optional:
Food circulars and magazines

Personal Memento Museum

What does your child cherish the most? You'll find out when you visit his or her personal memento museum.

First, designate a room to be used as a museum. Then, ask your child to select some of his or her favorite possessions (photos, drawings, toys, school projects). An older child might want to include awards, certificates, and trophies that he or she has won. The "curator" can divide his or her museum into "exhibit sections," with each devoted to a different theme (school, hobbies, and so on).

Have your child make a placard for each display (with a title and a brief description) and then prepare a script for a guided tour. As a museumgoer, you can ask questions about the displays or swap stories with the tour guide.

Who knows, maybe you'll finally learn the significance of that gum wrapper your child has been saving all these years . . .

Required:

Photos, drawings, toys, school projects and other possessions; awards, certificates and trophies; art supplies, cardboard or poster board

AT
HOME

Pick-Up Straws and More

Here are a couple of ways to recycle those straws that always seem to jam up the silverware drawers.

First, suggest the old favorite, pick-up sticks or, in this case, straws. The object of the game is to remove a straw from the pile without disturbing the rest of the straws. If the straws move, that player forfeits his or her turn. When the pile has been picked up, the player with the most straws wins. In a shorter version of the game, a player is eliminated when he or she disturbs the pile, and the winner is the remaining player.

When the game of pick-up straws is done, take just ten seconds to show your kids how to crease the end of a straw and insert it into the open end of another. By bending and creasing, kids can create all kinds of artistic shapes, as well as people, cars, etc. Be sure to supply thread so your kids can hang their straw art in the kitchen—then you'll have a galley turned gallery!

Required:

Drinking straws, thread

Do your children love getting postcards from friends and relatives traveling in exciting and exotic places? Have them create their own postcards to mail from an imaginary journey.

Supply your children with five-by-seven-inch index cards for the blank postcards and have them add pictures to the front and greetings on the back. They can draw original pictures or glue on photos cut from magazines to depict their imaginary travel destinations, complete with descriptions and notes about their activities. Have them finish their postcards by adding pretend postage stamps.

You can also have your children make a mailbox to mail their postcards from (the role of mail carrier would be an excellent one for a younger child to play). Older children can actually mail their postcards; make sure that addresses are legible and that all glued-on pieces are secure first.

Having a wonderful time, wish you were here!

Required:

Writing and art supplies, index cards, magazines or other photo sources, nontoxic glue

AT
HOME

If you're making a special birthday meal, this game can be played by several kids at once. Not only does it give them something to do while you cook, but it adds to the "party" atmosphere.

The game is modeled after "Pin the Tail on the Donkey." To play, your kids cut out pictures of food from grocery ads, food circulars, or magazines. Then they stick a small loop of tape to the back of each picture. Finally, they attach a paper plate to the refrigerator with tape. Now they're ready to play.

Each player takes a food picture, closes his or her eyes, then tries to place that picture on the plate. After all the pictures have been placed, kids can have fun talking about the crazy meal and the messy placemat their jumbled plate would make.

Required:

Art supplies, paper plate, food pictures, magnetic letters (for variation)

A quick alternative to this game, if you have a fridge covered with magnetic letters, is to dump the letters in a hat, have kids close their eyes, draw the letters, and place them on the fridge. What words can they make from the jumbled letters? Hey, that spells fun!

Kids love the way Ping-Pong balls sound when they bounce them. Why not add some simple targets and give them something to shoot for?

Paper bags, tall plastic cups, empty frozen-juice containers, and shoeboxes all make great kid-safe targets. (Stuffing paper towels in the bottom of the targets will help keep the balls from escaping.) Your kids can shoot for a single target at a time, for multiple targets in a line, or for targets randomly scattered around a room.

They can also try to get the Ping-Pong balls into the targets in a single bounce, or they can specify the number of bounces each throw must take. And they can make the game more challenging by trying to bounce the balls over obstacles like a wall of blocks or a piece of string tied between two chairs. For younger children, make the targets larger and have them simply toss the Ping-Pong balls into them.

Want a really silly game? Change the targets to things like one of Dad's shoes, a cup of water, or a cereal bowl (skip the milk).

Required:

Ping-Pong balls, paper bags, tall plastic cups, empty frozen-juice containers, shoeboxes

Here are some more quick ideas for using a Ping-Pong ball for kitchen entertainment.

First have your kids try a little warm-up exercise—seeing how long they can bounce a Ping-Pong ball inside a sauce pan. Then see if your kids can bounce a Ping-Pong ball and then catch it in a small strainer. Or put the ball into a muffin tin and have the players try to roll the ball from cup to cup.

When everyone's worn out, they can try their hand at "carousel," which entails placing a Ping-Pong ball in a large bowl. The players then take turns rotating the bowl so that the ball rolls along the sides. The faster they turn the bowl, the higher the ball rises on the side. How far and fast can it go without shooting out? NASA calls this exit speed "escape velocity," but these Ping-Pong challenges will more than likely keep your kids happily in the kitchen orbit.

Required:

Saucepans, strainer, muffin tin, Ping-Pong ball, large bowl

Place Maps

There's nothing like a good map to keep you on course when you're traveling. And there's nothing like a good "place map" when your kids are setting the table. The place map shows your table setters exactly what should be placed on the table for each person, and where it should go.

During a lull in the cooking, set a regular place setting. Then help your child trace each element—the silverware, plate, cup, napkin, etc.—on a large piece of paper (about eleven by sixteen inches). Older kids can copy the map, making one for each member of the family. Your younger kids can help too, by coloring in the tracings. Cover the place maps with clear self-adhesive wrap, and your place *maps* will become nifty place *mats*.

Now, when the youngest kitchen helpers go to set the table, they only have to place the plates, glasses, and silverware where the place mats show them to. No more guesswork, and no more missing forks!

Required:

Large sheets of paper, art supplies, clear adhesive covering

AT
HOME

Your kitchen has just been transformed into a world-class laboratory. And the experiment is one of great concern to humankind!

For this kitchen chemistry experiment, place one ice cube in each of five small unbreakable bowls. Then have your child sprinkle the ice cubes with the following: flour, rice, a spice, salt, and corn starch (you can use anything you want, as long as one of the items is actually salt, and the other items contain little or no salt).

Now ask your child to observe if any of the items sprinkled on the ice cubes seem to affect how fast they melt. The salted ice cube will melt the fastest, because the salt lowers the freezing point.

Required:

Salt, cereals, rice, and other common foods; ice cubes; small bowls

Have your child experiment with other "melting agents," such as cereal, sugar, or other ingredients in your cupboard. Who knows—your child might come up with an environmentally sound way to melt ice and feed the birds at the same time.

Predictions

How well do you know your children? How well do they know you? Here's a guessing game that will help you find out.

The essence of this game is the "Food Test," which your child creates with ten questions. (What's your favorite vegetable? Which fruit do you think has the most seeds? What breakfast food is Aunt Betsy's specialty? and so on.)

To play, your child writes down his or her predictions about how you'll answer the Food Test questions. Then your child quizzes you, so he or she can see how well the predictions panned out.

If your younger child needs help coming up with the questions for the "Food Test," give him or her a hand. But keep your answers to yourself until your child makes his or her best guesses.

Required:
Writing supplies

Who knows? You might find out that your kids really do like broccoli and cauliflower. Those sounds they make whenever you serve them are just expressions of joy!

There's nothing like a finger-painting session to help your young child pass the time while you're cooking. Especially when the paint is actually pudding—it feels good under their hands, and it's just messy enough to appeal to kids!

Before your next cooking session, whip up a batch of vanilla pudding. Then when it's time to make dinner, offer your kids the pudding/paint, as well as sheets of wax paper set in the bottom of a cookie sheet. You can also provide some empty yogurt containers and food coloring, so your finger painters can mix small batches of custom-colored pudding. Then turn your kids loose to create their pudding artwork!

Required:

Vanilla pudding, food coloring, yogurt containers, kitchen implements

While your children will likely want to get their hands into the thick of it, you can also supply a variety of "painting" tools, such as spoons, melon ballers, butter knives, and other utensils that your child can use to mold and shape the pudding.

You can be certain of one thing: This is one project where the art might truly look good enough to eat!

Quick Mimes

Can your child convey a wealth of meaning through physical gestures alone? Have him or her pantomime some of the following (without props):

- Walking, feeding, and playing with a pet dog
- Getting dressed, brushing teeth and hair, and leaving for school
- Unwrapping birthday presents and blowing out the candles on a cake
- Picking flowers and arranging them in a vase
- Cooking dinner, setting the table, and serving the meal
- Playing a game of tennis, baseball, soccer, etc.
- Collecting shells at the seashore, taking a dip in the ocean, and building sandcastles

Your child can also choose his or her own actions to mime, and you can guess what he or she is doing. Of course, you can try some mimes yourself. How does it feel to ride an invisible covered wagon over the Continental Divide?

AT
HOME

Here's an easy art project that can lead to an on-going fun and educational family activity: a framed holder for posting tidbits and trivia. Your child can use it to display a "quote of the day," "word of the day," or notes from "this day in history."

The frame itself is simple to make. Cut a rectangle out of the front side of a large envelope, leaving a one-inch border all the way around, and have your child decorate it, including a title for the selected category. Next, punch a hole through the front end and the flap so nothing will fall out when it's hung up. Each new quote, word, or other interesting tidbit can be written on a clean piece of paper and put in the envelope so it shows through the frame.

Your child can look for quotes in the newspaper or in favorite books, encyclopedias, and dictionaries; for variety he or she can make up original quotes, silly words, or historical nonevents.

Say, this is fun; you can quote us on that.

Required:

Large envelope; scissors; art and writing supplies; newspapers, books and other print sources

Rainbow Cubes

Nothing brightens up a cabin-bound day like a rainbow. If none are handy, your child can make one in the comfort of your kitchen.

Adult Supervision

Fill an ice-cube tray *partway* with water (you don't want the water overflowing the individual compartments). Then, have your children add food coloring to the water; a drop per cube is plenty. Encourage your child to be adventurous and mix and blend the colors. (Remember that concentrated food coloring can stain furniture, so work on newspapers and break out the painting smocks.)

Place the tray back in the freezer and allow the water to freeze. Remove the frozen cubes and place them in a plastic bowl or dish for observation (not for use in drinks); as the cubes melt, the colors will stream and swirl, adding to the fun.

Required:
Ice-cube trays, food coloring, plastic container

For a fancier frozen rainbow, your child can layer colored ice in a plastic container. Color about half an inch of water in the container at a time, allowing it to freeze before adding the next layer.

Whatever colors your child chooses, the rainbows are certain to brighten up the day.

Time to get your kitchen organized. And you can start—or get your kids to start–by putting some order to that box of jumbled recipes you've been storing in the pantry.

The first step to getting your recipe file together is to make up categories for the recipes. Your kids can do this on their own with index cards, such as "Yummy Desserts," "Fancy Sunday Meals," "Humble Hamburger," "Dad's Favorites," "Quick Meals for Mom," and "Kid Specialties." Kids write the name of the category on top and then illustrate the name with a picture. They don't have to be absolutely literal here. "Dad's Favorites" can picture Dad's hungry face, or a smiling dad patting a very full stomach.

Required:

Index cards, art supplies

If they prefer, kids can organize the dividers by food groups or main ingredients. They may need your help if you want your recipes filed in a certain way, but if you're happy with anything that reduces the clutter, this activity will do the trick!

You might even find that chicken dish you've been wondering about for the last six months!

Recombinant Foods

What do you get when you cross a carrot and an apricot? Why, a caricot, of course!

Have your child imagine that he or she can combine various foods and create new ones. For instance, your child can combine two fruits, name the new fruit, tell you what it tastes like, describe it, and draw a picture of it. He or she can cross two vegetables, desserts, spices, etc.

As a variation, have your child develop a list of ingredients composed completely of "recombinant foods." For example, the list can include caricots, limeas (lima beans and peas), tunalmon (tuna and salmon), waterloupe (watermelon and cantaloupe), and walcans (walnuts and pecans). Then your child can create a recipe using those ingredients—for example, Very Strange Tunalmon Casserole!

Optional:
Art supplies

Your child can then draw the recipe and add it to his or her homemade cookbook. So what do you get when you cross a creative kid with a fun activity?

The Rosetta stone enabled eighteenth-century scholars to decipher the hieroglyphics' of ancient Egypt by providing "parallel" passages in Greek and Egyptian. You can invent your own Rosetta stones right in your living room, and you won't even need a hammer and chisel.

Take a piece of paper and list all the letters of the alphabet in a column. Next to each letter, place a different geometrical shape, arrow, simple picture, or other visual substitute.

Now write out a message using the "graphic alphabet," hand your child the translation sheet, and see if he or she can read the correct words.

And for a hotshot code buster, try this: Leave about three quarters of the letters as they are but substitute graphics and symbols for the rest. Write out a message in the "hybrid" alphabet and see if your child can crack the code *without* a translation sheet.

S*! %L?*S? *:^ @*:K !0*

(Which means: Enjoy this activity!)

Required:

Writing supplies

Sandwich Bag Designers

Who says brown sandwich bags have to be boring? Here's an activity that your kids can do to give their sandwich bags a new look.

Supply paper sandwich bags, art supplies, glitter, and glue to open your "brown bag factory." Your kids can decorate the bags with original drawings, glue on sequins, affix self-adhesive stars, and the like. Another approach they can take is to imitate a drawing from a favorite storybook or an encyclopedia. Or they might cut out pictures from old magazines, catalogs, and junk mail (nothing like a picture of T-rex to conjure up the image of a voracious appetite). For an added touch, supply self-adhesive Velcro strips that your children can affix to the top of the bags.

Who knows? Your kids might start a great trend in school when they sport their custom-made designer lunch gear!

Required:

Paper bags, art supplies, glitter, nontoxic glue

AT
HOME

They know what it looks like. They know what it tastes like. They can even tell it by the aroma. But do your kids *really* know what goes into their favorite dish?

Test their food knowledge in a fun way by writing down the ingredients from two recipes, with each ingredient on a separate strip of paper. Then tell your kids what the finished dishes are supposed to be. The object is for your kids to separate the ingredients into two piles, one for each recipe. (An alternate version for pre- or early readers is to get out the actual ingredients and see if they can group them by recipes).

You can increase the challenge in several ways. Try using more than two recipes. Or, don't tell your kids the names of the dishes and see if they can figure out the intended results. Finally, try using similar recipes—cupcakes and banana bread, for example.

There's no penalty for guessing wrong—unless you want to let your kids eat the recipes they put together.

Required:

Recipes, writing supplies

Scrap Stamp Painting

Do your kids love to paint? If so, here's a new way to apply their artistry. All your children need to create some original artwork is tempera paint, paper, and a collection of found objects to use as stamps. Almost anything will do: film canisters, foam packing peanuts, erasers, crumpled paper, paper clips. They can even roll toy cars through the paint to make tire tracks or use plastic animals to make footprints.

Pour the paint into dishes or plastic lids wide enough for the objects selected and supply each of your children with a large sheet of paper. They can stick with abstract designs or take inspiration from the first shape they put on the paper to create their picture (a circle can become a head, a square or rectangle can be the start of a city, or a splotch from a piece of sponge can become a wave crashing on a beach). Your children can also use more conventional tools (brushes and fingers) to complete their paintings.

Required:
Art supplies, recycled materials, small objects, toys

What to do when their masterpieces are done and dried? The kids can stage their very own art show in the playroom gallery.

Feel like pampering yourself? Then pay a visit to your home beauty salon and let your child transform you into a model.

First, have your child furnish his or her beauty parlor with a real or pretend sink (a box), mirror, hair dryer, chairs, etc. Style supplies (clips, ponytail holders, barrettes, headbands, and so on) should also be stocked. Choose your treatment (new style, shampoo, coloring, or whatever); you and your child may find unusual hairstyles to duplicate in magazines or newspapers, or your child can work from your directions or pure imagination.

Of course, your child's beauty services might also extend to other areas, such as manicures, massages, facial masks, and makeup. In fact, why not ask for an entire makeover; with your child's skills, you'll surely be the talk of the town.

Required:

Large cardboard box; hair dryer and mirror (or make-believe equivalents); clips, ponytail holders, barrettes, headbands, and other hair accessories

Shooting Hoops

Here's a way to have some basketball fun in your living room. You don't need a ball and you don't need a basket; here's how to make your own.

For a ball, use a mesh onion bag filled with wadded-up newspaper and held closed with a rubber band or knotted string. Crumple the newspapers loosely so that they fill up the onion bag.

To make a basket, double up two large paper bags, fold the tops down two to three times in one-inch folds for stiffness, and cut the bottoms out. You may want to add a strip of duct tape around the top for added strength. Then attach the bag to the back of a chair, either with masking tape or string laced through small holes punched in the top strip, and you're ready to begin the game.

Have your children start by seeing how many baskets they can get in ten throws from a fixed line. As their shooting improves, you can have them try more challenging games, like taking a step back after each successful shot they make. With a bit of practice and a change of weather, you'll be ready to take the Living Room Trotters for their debut in the big league.

Required:

Mesh onion bag, newspapers, rubber band or string, large paper bags, duct tape, masking tape, string

AT
HOME

Setting the table is one of the first chores that many kids perform for the family. This activity will add a new twist to the task, and a new accoutrement to your kitchen—a silverware organizer.

Your child starts by covering a shoebox with paper, then decorates it with art supplies. He or she then tapes a lengthwise cardboard divider inside the box (made from the lid) to create two long compartments. Along one side of the box, glue or tape toilet paper tubes standing in place (trim the height first so they are flush with the top of the box—your job). The tubes can hold silverware, and the rest of the organizer can be used for napkins, the salt and pepper shakers, and other light items.

Required:

Shoebox, toilet paper tubes, sheet of cardboard, art supplies, tape or nontoxic glue, stapler

To make a handle, take two strips of cardboard the length of the box and about one inch wide. Staple the ends of the double-thickness cardboard to the center of the long sides of the box (overlap the side of the box by at least two inches to provide ample area for stapling).

Now if you could create a device to make clearing the table so easy!

Cooking and cutting and mixing in the kitchen—
even a pretend one—are a lot of fun for kids.
But where do your kids clean the resulting make-
believe mess?

At the play sink, of course. To make the sink,
tape both ends of a large carton shut. Then, give
your kids a plastic dishpan. After they trace
around the top of the pan on one side of the box,
cut it out for them (make sure it's slightly smaller
than the rim, so the edge will support the rim).
Your kids can use the sink dry or with a small
amount of water, if you're comfortable with the
idea.

To make faucets, cut three holes behind the
sink, each just wide enough to accommodate a
toilet paper or paper towel tube. Insert a paper
towel tube for the spigot (middle hole), then cut a
wedge about three inches wide from the end protruding, bend the tube over, and tape in place. Insert a toilet paper tube in the holes on either side
for the faucets.

Say, is that a tiger in the kitchen? No, it's just
your child impersonating the disposal.

Required:

*Dishpan or
shallow box,
large carton,
toilet paper or
paper towel
tubes, tape,
art supplies*

Coming face-to-face with a three-hundred-pound, people-eating carrot would make anybody go goggle-eyed. That won't happen in your kitchen, of course—until you plug into your child's imagination.

As you chop food for the evening's meal, get your children thinking about what it would be like to strap on some scuba gear and go diving into a giant bowl of soup. As they begin their journey, they can tell you their adventures and the sights they see.

Feel free to jump in when your child slows down. You might say something about skirting a chunk of broccoli the size of a house. Or suggest sitting on a pea to enjoy the chunks of pepper drifting by.

Soup isn't the only dish that's fun to explore, of course. What about spelunking in fowl caves—venturing into the cavity of a big turkey or chicken that you're preparing to roast. Or, how about scaling the side of a ham? Watch out: Fall into the gravy boat, and you're as good as cooked!

Spoon Ball

Keeping two kids occupied while you make dinner requires some special thinking—and a couple of spoons.

In this game, each player gets a soup spoon. The object is for your kids to pass a Ping-Pong ball from spoon to spoon without dropping it.

After they master the basic skills, they can try passing the ball while walking across the kitchen. Or they can score extra points with the audience (that's you) with fancy passes behind the back, between the legs, or over the shoulder. If your kids get really good at the game, they might even try it blindfolded. If three kids are playing, the two passers can play blindfolded while the third player directs them.

Required:
Ping-Pong ball, spoons

Finally, if you have an interesting tile pattern, your kids can establish certain "bounce" zones—places where it's OK to drop the ball, and places where it will be gobbled up by a shark—that should add some tension to the game.

Just one thing, don't get too caught up in the laughter—you might find yourself with an unexpectedly crispy meal!

This simple ball-toss activity will have your children doing some quick arithmetic while having quick fun.

The object of the game is to toss a rubber ball up a flight of stairs so it bounces back, hitting as many steps as possible on the way down. Before the game, the players print numbers on sheets of paper and tape them to the front of each step to indicate the point value.

Each player stands at the bottom of the stairs and tosses the ball up. As the ball comes back down, the player adds up the numbers assigned to the steps it bounces on; the more bounces the higher the score.

Required:

Writing supplies, tape, rubber ball

For a more challenging game, alternate between two different colors of paper on the steps, designating one as "add points" and the other as "subtract points." Younger children can enjoy the game as well by simply counting the number of bounces.

OK, get set to watch the bouncing ball . . .

Here's a version of bingo sure to inspire a beginning reader or group of players while generating a few belly laughs.

Make bingo cards by drawing a four-by-four-square grid (for a total of sixteen squares) on a piece of blank paper or thin cardboard. Ask the players to list common words that you or they can write in the squares. Stick with words that appear frequently in children's storybooks, such as "for," "yes," "I," "go," "boy," and "girl." Be sure that the children place the words randomly so that every card is different.

Have the players cut bingo markers out of colored paper with safety scissors, then begin reading a selected story. The children then listen for the words on their cards and place a marker on each word that they hear. The first one who places four markers on his or her card in a straight line in any direction shouts *bingo!* When that happens, remove the markers, swap cards, and get back to the story.

Required:

Writing supplies, white paper or thin cardboard, colored paper, safety scissors, favorite books

Here's a new twist on a scavenger hunt that young readers will have fun with as they follow clues from their favorite books. Lead your children to a hidden prize by giving them written clues that rely on books with which they're familiar and you have in your home. Each clue should relate to something from one of the familiar books to lead your child to an object in your home. For example:

Goldilocks sat on one on page 10 could be a hint to look on the rocking chair for the next clue.

Madeline was in one on page 23 might lead your kids to a bed.

Look for something the color of Max's boat could direct them to a red piece of paper after they check in Sendak's classic *Where the Wild Things Are*.

Required:

Books, writing supplies, prize or treat

Older children can use magazines and newspapers. For younger kids, simply give them the clues, directing them to picture books that they know very well.

Any ideas for a clue from *Harold and the Purple Crayon*? That should lead to some interesting places . . .

Stove Timer Hunt

Time is running out and the banana is still missing! One or more kids can play this rousing version of "Beat-the-Clock." Hide an object in the kitchen, then set the timer for a specified period of time (say, five minutes).

For young children, choose large objects and hide them in plain view. If you have older children, you can make the game more sophisticated by using smaller objects, making the hiding places more difficult, or setting the timer for a shorter period.

This game is great for one child, but it can be played by two or more as well. Kids can play as teams, or they can compete against one another. If they play against one another, try calling them into the kitchen one by one, and hide the object in the same place for each player. Or, if you need to be free to cook, have one child do the hiding and the other child (or children) be the seekers.

Required:

Kitchen timer, objects to hide

Now, where is that spatula? It was here just a second ago!

If your kids enjoyed Pick-Up Straws and More (see activity 124), set them up with the following games, then get back to your pot stirring.

First try "kitchen chemist." Your child dips a straw into a bowl of water, puts a finger over the open end, then transfers the liquid into the ice tray compartments. Try adding a few drops of food coloring to the water to give the activity more of an "official laboratory" or "mad scientist" feel.

How about "indoor plumbers"? Set your egg timer and then see if your plumber/child can move all of the water from bowl one to bowl two before the time expires, using only a straw. Got a big plumbing task? Break out the giant punch bowl (plastic, please)!

Finally, there's "Kitchener's Travels." See how many objects your kids can identify in the kitchen while closing one eye and using a straw as a spyglass. Have them imagine that they're Lilliputians and the straws are mighty telescopes. How does the world look from that perspective?

Required:

Drinking straws, ice cube tray, bowls, food coloring

Why not have your child serve a formal meal to some special guests while you're cooking? It shouldn't be much trouble, as long as you choose the right dinner guests.

Ask your child to invite some of his or her stuffed animals to a banquet in a restaurant. Your child can make place cards and place mats for each guest, and then set the table with dishes, silverware, napkins, and cups. The host (your child) might also make menus listing something for each stuffed animal: honey for the teddy bear, carrots for the bunny, flies for the frog, etc.

The stuffed animals, with some help from your child, can then take their places around the table. Your child shifts into waiter mode to take orders from the furry guests, then serve them and make sure that everything is up to the animals' standards.

Required:

Your child's stuffed animals, art supplies

When the stuffed animals are satisfied, perhaps your child can join them and partake of the elegant feast. Hmm, your child could actually learn to enjoy chocolate-covered cricket legs!

AT
HOME

Silly stuffed-animal tricks? You bet, and they're all on tape in your video camera.

Have your child gather several of his or her stuffed animals (if possible, choosing the most talented of the lot). Then give your child a chance to rehearse various acts with the creatures. Perhaps Teddy can walk on a rolling ball and Babar the elephant can do somersaults, back flips, handstands, and other gymnastic exercises, despite his size.

Get the camera ready, cue your child, then let the tape roll while the "performers" go through their paces. Your child can also explain to the video audience how he or she trained the animals, and give the creatures' names and backgrounds.

And don't worry if the "talent" makes a mistake or two on the air; that's to be expected in a live production.

Required:

Video camera, stuffed animals

Subminiature Golf

Here's a plan for big fun with a small version of an old family favorite. It's miniature golf with marbles and Popsicle sticks instead of golf balls and putters.

Your children can use the Popsicle sticks as is for putters, or they can glue on a shorter piece of stick or a rectangle of hard foam for the putter head. Use a large piece of corrugated cardboard for the golf course (two or more pieces can be taped together to get the desired size) and place it on several uniformly tall boxes to elevate it off the floor. Then cut holes in it slightly larger than the diameter of the marbles (remember, marbles may not be suitable for younger children).

Have your children add decorations (perhaps paint the areas around the holes green) and obstacles to the course. Obstacles can include cardboard tubes to putt through, blocks for bumpers, and, of course, plastic animals, figurines, and plastic dinos or space people to create the feel of a true miniature golf course.

Adult Supervision

Required:

Marbles, Popsicle sticks, corrugated cardboard boxes

Optional:

Hard foam sheets, double-stick tape or non toxic glue, cardboard tubes, small toys, paint, blocks

AT
HOME

You and your child can enjoy doing the food shopping together, especially when the supermarket is in your own home.

Have your child create a grocery store, complete with various departments: fruits and vegetables, the freezer section, the deli counter, and so on. Your child can draw food items or cut pictures from magazines and supermarket circulars for the grocery stock. Empty cardboard boxes can represent "packaged" goods (pasta, cereals, etc.). Be sure to make play currency too.

Once your child has stocked the supermarket with his or her favorite foods, you can select some products by putting them into a basket, bag, or box. And, while you're shopping, your child can conduct taste tests, sell you on a new food, or demonstrate a new recipe.

Finally, head over to the cash register and let your child ring up your order. Then, you can have your child switch roles with you and take a whirl at shopping—provided you've left any food on the shelves, that is!

Required:

Food products (or their empty containers); magazines and supermarket circulars; scissors; basket, bag, or box

Optional:

Play currency, cooking and serving supplies

Is your family on a lucky streak? Then have your child enter each family member in a homespun lottery.

Your child can make a variety of prizes such as drawings, modeling-clay sculptures, greeting cards, and poems. (Make sure he or she makes enough items so that everybody gets one.) Then have your child write the prize names on slips of paper (one prize per slip) and put each in a separate envelope. Mix up the envelopes and place one under each family member's dinner plate.

Instead of homemade prizes, older children might substitute "service coupons" (slips of paper that entitle the bearer to such gifts as "breakfast in bed," "reading a story," and "closet cleaning"). The recipient gets to decide on a time to redeem the prize.

Required:
Art and writing supplies, envelopes

After dinner (or at another appropriate time when the rest of the family is at home), have participants take turns opening the envelopes and reading their prizes aloud. Your child can present the homemade gifts and elaborate on the service prizes. Isn't it great when everyone is a winner?

Here's a version of basketball in which someone seven feet tall would be at an extreme disadvantage!

Before you cook, help your kids create two "nets" (just make one if a single child will be playing). Take a piece of stiff cardboard and cut a hole in it slightly smaller in diameter than the rim of a paper cup (the mouth of the cup should be at least two inches in diameter). Slip the cup through the hole in the cardboard, so that the rim rests on the cardboard. Now place the cardboard at the edge of the table, with the cup extending over the edge. Place a book or other heavy object on the edge of the cardboard so that it doesn't obstruct the cup (see illustration). Repeat the process for the second "net" and place it at the opposite end of the table.

Required:

Sheet of cardboard, two paper cups, Ping-Pong balls, books or other heavy objects

The players then bounce or roll a Ping-Pong ball across the table, trying to land it in each other's net. They can score the game as in traditional basketball, or invent their own system.

When you get a break in the cooking, you might want to demo your famous hook shot. Wow—what a dunk!

Tabletop Playhouse

While you're busy in your kitchen, your child can be running a household of his or her own using cartons, containers, and utensils for props— it only takes imagination!

Have your child pick out a few favorite dolls or play figures to bring to the table, then supply kitchen objects to create the playhouse. Help your child start by selecting some items that fit well with the play figures he or she has selected. Your child can, for example, use a loaf pan as a crib for a doll, spice boxes for chairs, and a cracker box for a table. A rectangular box can make for a good refrigerator (cut a door), and a square box can serve as a stove (cut a door for the oven).

And for the backyard? How about a miniature playground with a swiveling serving tray for a merry-go-round and a potato masher for a swing!

Why, in no time at all your kitchen table will be transformed into a veritable palace!

Required:

Cartons, containers, utensils, play figures

AT
HOME

Adult Supervision

This activity adds a new swing to bowling. Instead of rolling a ball to try to knock over the pins, your child swings a Wiffle or foam ball suspended from a string.

To start, you need to prepare a ball for hanging in a doorway from a long piece of string. If you're using a foam ball, push a needle and thread through the surface and tie it in a loop to connect the string (your job). Attach the string to the top of the door frame with packaging tape or a thumbtack so that the ball hangs about two inches above the floor.

When the ball setup is complete, have your child place one or more toilet paper tubes on the floor and try to knock them over by gently swinging the ball at them.

For variety, suggest the following: arranging the targets in different patterns, stacking them in pyramids, or even lining them up close to each other and trying to knock over just one tube at a time.

One thing is certain: Once your child gets in the swing of this game, he or she will truly have a ball.

Required:

String, Wiffle or foam ball (foam ball requires needle and thread), thumbtack or tape, toilet paper tubes

Thar She Blows!

Here's a variety of tabletop "air games" that put some old Ping-Pong balls to good use.

First try "air hockey." Set two plastic cups or yogurt containers on their sides at opposite ends of the table. Then provide drinking straws for each player and explain that the object is to get the ball into the other person's goal by blowing on it through the straw. (You might want to tape the cups to the table to keep them from moving.) For cooperative play, kids can set up a single goal, then help each other maneuver the ball into the goal.

How about "puff-a-war," the straw version of tug-of war? Two players sit on opposite sides of the table, separated by a divider line (a string, a piece of tape, etc.). Place the Ping-Pong ball on the line. Each player tries to blow the ball off the other player's side of the table.

Finally, there's "air discus," in which each player takes turns seeing who can make the Ping-Pong ball roll farthest with one blow.

Before long, your tabletop will be a whirlwind of fun!

Required:

Plastic straws, Ping-Pong ball, plastic cups or yogurt containers

AT
HOME

When is a cooking pot not a cooking pot? When it's a window on another world.

Cut pieces of paper so they'll fit snugly inside various pots and pans. Hand your child the pieces of paper and some art supplies so he or she can decorate the paper. The pots, when set on their sides, will become a series of "portholes" into an imaginary or faraway place.

For instance, each pot or pan might have an undersea scene. One could show a certain type of fish, another a sunken ship, and another a scuba diver. Or the pots might depict adventures in the jungle, life inside a dollhouse, or your child's version of a storybook.

Required:

Pots and pans, art supplies

When your child has decided on a theme and finished the drawings, place the papers back in their respective pots (you might need a small piece of masking tape rolled in a loop to affix them), and have him or her describe the scenes, taking you from pot to pot, and pan to pan.

Phew! It's a good thing those tigers are out there and not here in the kitchen!

Tile Olympics

How would you like to gain some points for something besides your cooking? Simply turn the kitchen floor into a giant scoreboard, and your kids can rack up as many points as they'd like.

Small Parts!

Provide several flat objects, such as pennies or buttons, that fit easily in the squares or diamonds or other shapes that make up your floor tile. Then help your children turn the floor into a target; all of the tiles above a horizontal row might be worth five points, while all those below it might be worth ten. Or you can assign points to the tiles in "checkerboard" fashion; every other tile might be good for five points, and the tiles in between might be worth ten. In either case, a special "bull's-eye" tile might be worth twenty points.

Players take turns pitching the pennies or buttons and tallying their points. For an even greater challenge, your kids can toss a Ping-Pong ball and see where it finally comes to rest.

Required:

Pennies or buttons, or Ping-Pong ball

Ready, everyone? Then let the Tile Olympics begin!

Just because they're sitting at the table doesn't mean kids can't take a trip. All they need is a map of their own! Cover the table with paper and provide art supplies, then suggest various elements that they might add to their surface map, like a lake, a river with a bridge, a forest, and roadways.

At the street level, your kids can add small squares to represent houses and buildings. They can also sketch in the office where you or your spouse work, their school, the library, and other important buildings.

Younger kids can bring in cars and figures and turn the drawing into a real tabletop town; older kids can continue the cartography by drawing a legend (e.g., circles represent trees, rectangles represent cars), directional indicators, and key statistics about the town (population, date founded, historical points, and so on).

This is one map you don't have to worry about folding: Just roll it up for a rainy day!

Required:

Paper or bags for covering table, art supplies

Optional:

Toy cars and figures

The aroma of cooking food works magic on any appetite. And while the cooking is going on, this inventive game weaves its own spell in your kitchen.

Ask your child to join you at the counter as you prepare the meal. As you cut and chop, pretend the two of you are magicians preparing a magic potion. Look at the food with a child's eyes—soon you'll be stirring vulture eggs into the corn bread!

Your spice rack can be an especially enchanting vault of spells and sorcery: Here's a sprinkle of lion hair and a dash of shark tooth. Be sure to describe the effects of each ingredient as well as the power of the overall brew. Call out a few official-sounding magician's words for added effect.

Shazam! Kazoom! The ultimate spaghetti sauce—it turns ordinary silverware into gold, broccoli into chocolate chip cookies, and tired kids into energetic and happy cleaner-uppers and homework-doers!

Small Parts!

You might not see these tong games in the next Olympics. But you can count on them providing Olympic-sized fun for your kids.

Provide each player with a set of tongs (salad, barbecue, pasta, etc.). Then suggest that, using the tongs, your kids try passing around an object, say a small toy, or an empty plastic spice bottle. Too easy? See if they can hand off a small un-cooked noodle, a plastic milk jug lid, or a bean. Still too easy? How about a single grain of rice?!!

When a collection of items has been passed from one person to the next, see if everyone can pass the same object in the opposite direction without dropping anything. Or, for older kids, see whether they can play a speeded-up version—with their eyes closed! (Monitor to ensure safety.)

Required:

Tongs, common household/ kitchen items

Hey, after doing this activity enough times, your kids might be ready to help NASA train astronauts for in-space docking maneuvers!

Towel Trick

You know how to cook up a little magic in the kitchen; now your kids can try their own hand at some prestidigitation.

This trick is similar to the old tablecloth routine that you and your kids have seen in the old movies. In that trick, the magician whisks a tablecloth from a table without disturbing the items on the table. This version is considerably safer.

First, your child spreads a dish towel on top of the table or a free counter. Then, he or she sets some unbreakable objects on top of it. Freezer containers work great.

After a few magic words, your child tries to snatch off the dish towel without knocking anything onto the floor. He or she can embellish the trick with words to the "audience" like, "Tonight we have a very special treat in store for you," or "Straight from the magical palace of Wadoobee Fradoobee, the great dish towel trick!"

After your child masters this sleight of hand, he or she can work on making those dirty dishes magically disappear after dinner!

Required:
Dish towel, unbreakable objects

Kids get a kick out of following trail markers through the woods. This plan for an indoor hike gives your child a chance to follow the trail and to make new paths of his or her own. Best of all, he or she can be back in the kitchen for lunch or dinner.

You can mark the first trail for your hiker to follow by strategically placing socks as you weave along through rooms and hallways. Each sock should always be within sight of the previous one. Work with your child to create some simple rules, like having the toe of each sock always point to the next marker.

You can also add variety by turning the hike into a treasure hunt. Simply write clues on pieces of paper to put inside the socks that will direct your child to hidden treasures along the way: For example, "Proceed three more markers and find a large square object four paces from the trail."

Required:

Socks, writing supplies

Optional:

Prize or treat

After your explorer successfully follows your trail through the house, have him or her mark a route for you to follow. Now hit the trail, there's adventure ahead . . .

This activity, which allows your child to produce and talk back to TV shows, might be the only type of "interactive television" we'll ever endorse and enjoy.

To make some "tube head" gear, take a box at least twelve by twelve by eighteen inches and cut out a "screen" in front, as well as a hole in the bottom large enough for a person's head to comfortably fit through. Have your child draw a dial or two under the screen, or affix yogurt container lids; these are the "controls." In back of the "set," tape two drinking straws at a forty-five-degree angle to each other (the antennae).

Next, have your child make a TV listing, including the program titles and types (documentaries, cartoons, news, etc.) and segment descriptions. "Audience" members then take turns choosing the shows for your tube head child to "broadcast" (act out). For added fun, groups of kids can wear their own tube head gear and become part of the show.

This is one—and perhaps the only—time when you're sure to find "talking heads" great television!

Required:
large cardboard box, art supplies, yogurt container lids, nontoxic glue or tape, straws

Artists sometimes use castoff objects, old car parts, and an assortment of things otherwise destined for the junkyard to create their sculptures. Check out your recycling bin the next time your child is in the mood for a sculpting project.

Gather up cardboard tubes, chunks of foam, nonrecyclable containers, and paper, as well as glue and tape. For a simple and stable sculpture, a younger child can use a cardboard box as a base, then attach other objects to it with the glue and tape.

For additional fun, suggest that your child incorporate a marble chute into whatever sculpture piece he or she is creating (keep a close watch on younger siblings). Perhaps you'll be in the vanguard of a new art form: Art de Chute.

Whatever kinds of sculpture pieces your child makes, line them up in the playroom so everyone can enjoy a good old homemade sculpture garden.

Required:

Used containers, packing and other nonrecyclable materials, art supplies, nontoxic glue and tape

Two-Bit Tiddlywinks

Small Parts!

Tiddlywinks is an old favorite that involves snapping plastic disks into a target cup. Here's a do-it-yourself version that takes just small change to put together.

The idea of the game is to use a spoon to flip coins into a cup or bowl placed in the center of the table. Place the coins on the handle of a spoon, with the handle pointing away from the target. Gently tap the spoon so that the coin is launched into the air toward the target. After demonstrating how the launcher works, have the players experiment with different coins and different spoons to find the best combination.

For variety, add smaller and larger targets and assign a point value to each, the smaller the target the higher the points

One thing you can be sure of: Your children will flip when they get their two cents in!

Required:
*Coins, spoons,
cup or bowl*

Are your kids ready for a home of their own? Maybe not, but this simple on-the-wall dollhouse can make for some off-the-wall fun.

Begin by helping your children draw a cutaway view of a house on a large piece of paper. You can also have them draw outside scenery as viewed through the windows. When the house is ready, tape it to a wall and your junior interior decorators can get to work.

Have your children draw and color furniture, knickknacks, pets, and people to put in the house. They can try to make rooms that match their own homes or create the bedroom of their dreams. Encourage them to include small details to make their house look more like a home: dishes on the table, or a stack of magazines scattered on the coffee table, and so on.

How about that! Your kids not only made their bed, they made their whole house!

Required:

Large sheet of paper, art supplies, nontoxic glue, tape

What can you do in the kitchen with your whisk, potato masher, rubber spatula, and ice-cream scoop? *Why,* put on a puppet show, of course!

Your child can use the table as a stage. From "backstage" (under the table, actually), the puppeteer (or group of puppeteers) selects ordinary kitchen utensils and uses them to create various characters. For instance, a whisk, potato masher, and rubber spatula might become the Three Little Pigs, and an ice-cream scoop might become the Wolf. Other child-safe utensils that can be turned into puppets include spaghetti spoons, mushroom scrubbers, and melon ballers (how about turning them into zoo animals, prehistoric creatures, or a royal family?).

If your child needs additional characters, he or she can don oven mitts and turn them into instant puppets. With hands held horizontally, your child can make the mitt-puppets talk by moving his or her thumbs up and down.

Say, has anyone seen the apple corer? A cheese grater just stopped by to visit him!

Required:

Kitchen utensils, oven mitts

Here's a fun activity for your child to do while you're cutting fresh vegetables—you might call it "art you can eat!"

As you cut and chop, give your child the discarded vegetable pieces to assemble as a collage on a tray or plate. He or she might also draw the outline of a person's face, an animal, or an object, then use the vegetable pieces for features or details. Carrot ends, for instance, make wonderful eyes or wheels. For a vegetable landscape, your child can use small celery stalks to create a forest. The end of a cucumber will certainly make a fine nose or a mountain.

Required:

Vegetable trimmings, plate or tray

It helps if you cut the scraps into a variety of sizes and shapes, and you may want to include as well a few pieces that aren't scraps—broccoli florets, for instance, can make great hair for a vegetable head.

Whatever the outcome, you and your child are sure to agree that his or her picture is indeed very tasteful art!

Vegetable Printing

When you want to entertain your child in the kitchen, "play with your food" may be the order of the day, or in this case, "paint with your food!"

Vegetable stamps can be made by cutting potatoes or other root vegetables in half (your job). Cut around the design you wish to appear as a stamp, so that the design is left protruding from the surface of the root just like a regular ink stamp. A wide carrot is also a natural stamper; just cut off the bottom so you have a smooth surface to work from.

Brushes can be made from a variety of vegetables. A leafy celery stalk, for instance, is a natural paint brush. Broccoli florets, cauliflower, and string beans can also be used to paint, and will add interesting textures and patterns to the artwork.

Once the vegetables are ready, pour tempera paint into small containers. Your child can dip the vegetables in the paint and stamp pictures and patterns on the paper. Who knows—the results may be so exciting your child will try a few new vegetables!

Required:
Vegetables, tempera paint, paper

AT
HOME

It's not really surprising that Peter Pan never grew up, especially when you consider that Peter is a dancing stalk of celery!

With a few talented vegetables and some imagination, your child and other kitchen choreographers can stage a ballet right on the table. Suggest that your child and others use a familiar tale—say, *Peter Pan*—as a starting point, and then "cast" the principal roles. For example, a carrot might dance the part of Wendy, and a couple of pea pods might take on the characters of Michael and John.

The vegetables can skim and glide across the table to the songs or dialogue ad-libbed by the kitchen performers. Or, to increase the challenge, choreographers can try to convey the story using only vegetable dance steps.

Required:

Vegetables

Your child and his or her helpers might even stage a ballet while you guess which tale they're performing. Now, isn't it obvious that the radish is dancing the role of Little Red Riding Hood?

Video Biography

Isn't it nice to hear life stories of family members in their own words? Why not have your child conduct a biographical interview with siblings or friends? Here are some sample questions to begin with for younger and older subjects:

For Younger Subjects

Who's in your family? Who are your friends? What's your favorite playtime activity? Which books and songs do you like best? What is your favorite thing at school? Which color do you like the most?

For Older Subjects

Required:
Video camera

Were you named for anyone? Where did you grow up? What were your favorite things to do as a child? How have things changed since you were a child? What is the funniest thing that's ever happened to you? What advice can you give to others?

Encourage your child to think of more questions to ask, including follow-up questions during the interview. He or she can also create an autobiographical tape by answering the same interview questions on camera.

Take one!

AT
HOME

Congratulations! Your family has been selected to host the next Volume Olympics. And the main events will be held in your kitchen.

Have your kids gather together containers of various shapes and sizes. Then, they can guess which ones will hold more water. To see if they're right, they can use a measuring cup to pour water into the containers—over the sink, of course.

As a variation, see whether your children can line up the containers in sequence, from the one that will hold the most water to the one that will hold the least. Your kids can then use a measuring cup to find out if they were correct.

Yet another game involves thinking about volume equivalencies. Do two small plastic cups hold the same amount of water as one large cup? How about four medium cups—same as two large cups? Suggest various tests, then stand by for the results—they could be quite surprising!

Required:

Containers, measuring cups

Wacky Warm-Ups

Before your young athletes start any of their indoor sports events, get them properly warmed up with these silly stretches and crazy calisthenics. Remember, though, the main idea here is to stretch your kids' enjoyment!

To begin, pick someone to be the exercise leader (be sure to have the children change places often). Its the leader's task to come up with the stretches. Here are some starter ideas:

Finger flexes. "Fingers of both hands together; push and up and down. Again!"

Elbow flaps. "Strut like a chicken!"

Tongue stretches. "Stick out those tongues! You can do it; touch your nose!"

Eyebrow lifts. "Everyone together now; open your eyes WIDE and lift those lazy eyebrows!"

Toe wiggles. "Get those toes moving! Wiggle and waggle and spread and scrunch!"

Nostril flares. "Open and shut and open and shut!"

Moms and Dads, time to join the kids and S-T-R-E-T-C-H your fun too!

Wall Mural

Do you sometimes wish you had different views from the windows in your house? Why not have your kids create a trompe l'oeil wall mural of the vista of their choice? *Trompe l'oeil* means "fool the eye" in French, but in your playroom it means making a wall-sized picture, complete with door and windows through which some magnificent outdoor scenery is visible, like mountains or a rain forest.

Begin by taping pieces of paper together to form a larger sheet to tape to the wall. Have your kids decide what they want to draw, then perhaps start with a light pencil sketch of their idea before adding color. In addition to including a window or door on their mural, your children might add other details to make it look like part of the room.

Required:

Large sheets of paper, masking tape, art supplies

For instance, they can draw a picture on the picture, complete with a frame. They can also add touches like a crack in the wall, a light switch, or "paintings of paintings" and other artwork.

Or suggest this one: a magic button that, when pressed, will instantly clean up a playroom and make the sun come out!

All family members like a hearty welcome home, even if they've only been away for the school or work day, a half-hour errand, or a ten-minute excursion to shovel the walk.

Supply your child with large sheets of paper or poster board and art supplies to make welcome-home signs that can be placed near the door. For banners, provide a role of wide paper or have your child tape together sheets of paper or flat sections of paper bags.

Young children can draw pictures for the person who's been "away," while older kids can write greetings such as: "Hope you caught some rays while you were gone today." "We missed you so much while you went to the store!" "Hope you had fun during gym today."

Required:

Poster board or a roll of paper (or paper bags), art supplies

In any case, encourage silliness! The shorter the amount of time a particular person was away from the house, the more earnest should be the welcome message and greeting ritual. Speaking of which, welcome back from your walk around the block with the dog; everyone missed you a lot!

Here's a proven boredom buster designed for a child who enjoys dress-up games.

Gather some accessories (hats, gloves, jewelry, scarves, etc.), clothing (oversized shirts, socks, shoes, and the like), and a variety of props (a briefcase, a newspaper, sports equipment, and so on). Then have your child hop "onstage" (a space you designate for the performance). Now give your child an item or two. He or she can put on the "costume" (or hold it, if appropriate) and undergo a theatrical transformation.

Have your child introduce him- or herself, give basic facts (name, age, place of residence), and elaborate on his or her background. (Your child might also sing a song or tell a story in character.)

Required:

Costumes, props, accessories

You can ask the character questions to reveal additional information. And be sure to find out why he or she is wearing your child's favorite sweatshirt . . .

What's My Dish?

This rendition of an old game show won't earn anyone a refrigerator or trip to Las Vegas, but it's sure a great way to pass the time while you cook a meal.

To play, your child thinks of a food or completed dish. Then, you get to ask ten questions about it. Does it contain noodles? Is it Aunt Lynn's favorite dish? When would you eat this food? What other dishes does this taste good with?

After asking your ten questions, you have to guess the name of the food or meal. If you guess incorrectly, then your child gets to draw it. Now you can't miss guessing that the dish is tuna casserole with hot fudge sauce!

If you do guess correctly, then it's your turn to select the mystery food. If you're playing with very young children, keep your mystery food simple—an apple or banana, for example. The older the child, the more sophisticated the answers.

Kind of gives a whole new meaning to the phrase "mystery meal," doesn't it?

Kids love activities that challenge them to figure out what's misplaced in a picture. Here's a way to play the "What's Wrong Here?" game while you cook.

When you have a free moment, your child covers his or her eyes or leaves the room, and you put something in the wrong place. When your child returns or opens his or her eyes, you ask, "What's different in the kitchen?"

Then your child hunts around the room looking for the errant object. For a young child, keep it simple, like putting a banana in the silverware drawer. For an older child, try something more subtle, like slipping a box of rice among the boxes of cereal, or interspersing a can or two of cat food among the cans of tuna fish.

If your child is having trouble finding the location of the misplaced object, you can direct him or her by saying: "What's wrong with the cabinet?" Also, to add an element of suspense, set the timer and see if your child can figure out the puzzle before the buzzer goes off!

Although you and your child may not see eye to eye on every issue, you can still listen to each other's point of view. Choose a lighthearted "controversy," such as which pizza topping is best.

Have your child state and then back up his or her position (for example, perhaps your child favors pepperoni for its nice smooth edges). Counter his or her opinion with your own (you might tout the virtues of double-cheese: its calcium content, mellow flavor, and stringiness).

Give your child a chance to respond, then offer him or her a counterpoint, and so on. Are you ready to give the activity a twist? Switch positions with your child and begin again. See how well each of you can back up the "opposing" point of view (using original arguments or elaborating on each other's ideas).

Have either of you been swayed to the other camp's position on pizza toppings? Well, it is a child's (or is that "parent's"?) prerogative to change his or her mind.

Adult Supervision

Eye of newt, tongue of frog, turtle's breath, and moss from log. How come *imaginary* witches and magicians have all the fun? Your kids can concoct their own magic potions right in the kitchen.

Provide your kids with a variety of ingredients: spices, flour, cornstarch, pasta, ketchup, mustard, oil, cracker crumbs, stale bread, food coloring, vinegar, and baking soda (to add "fizz"). Also needed are bowls, spoons, a whisk, and measuring cups. Now turn them loose, and remember, the more disgusting their concoction the better!

Encourage your children to be "scientific" about their magic by measuring carefully and adding the ingredients at just the "right" time. To get in the true witches' brew spirit, ask them to describe their ingredients (mustard might be extract of bird feather) and the kind of magic the potion will make. Will it turn the cat into a dinosaur, make someone invisible, or melt a hole in the ground for a swimming pool?

Stir a bowl of gruesome mix, this witches' brew will work some tricks . . .

Required:

Common cooking ingredients, bowls, spoons, measuring cups, and other utensils

Would you believe that the sentence "The dog dug up his old bone from the yard, then brought it into the house for everyone to see" can be the source of great entertainment? All you need is a thesaurus or book of synonyms.

First, your child will need a list of sentences; make them up or cull them from magazines or books. Then provide the thesaurus and have your child try to find as many lofty-sounding replacements for the words in the sentence as possible. Take turns reading the sentences aloud and perhaps write the most intriguing on a large sheet of poster board or paper so other family members can enjoy them.

As a variation, have your child try to substitute haughty terms for the words in the first paragraph or two of a newspaper article, magazine story, or book. Either way, have your child read his or her versions aloud to you.

As for the sentence about Rover in the first paragraph above, try this: "The canine excavated his superannuated skeletal structure from the cloister garth, then transported it into the domicile for one and all to behold."

Required:

Thesaurus or synonym dictionary, writing supplies

Here's a game with a twist! Provide each child with one dry sponge (the sponges should be of roughly equal surface area) and a bowl. Pour the same amount of water into each bowl (the bowls should be in or near the sink, or next to a dishpan on some surface where water spillage won't cause problems). Set your timer and call out "Wring 'em!" The players then try to extract as much water as they can from their bowls with the sponge, wringing it into the sink or dishpan, before the timer goes off.

Also, encourage your kids to use the water from the game for the houseplants or garden, if appropriate.

Required:

Sponge, measuring cup, unbreakable bowls

A variation on this game involves having your kids conduct a joint effort to empty a dishpan with their sponges into other bowls before the timer goes off. That's good practice for the next time the sump pump in your basement goes!

Some people think that commercial television is pretty zany as it is, with inane plots that appear to be written by a visitor from another planet and commercials designed to transform our children into toy and junk-food addicts.

Adult Supervision

But there's hope if you produce your own "Cabin-Fever Television Special." Cut out a square from a large box (an appliance box works well, or set up four chairs in a square, drape an expendable sheet over them, and cut out the picture "screen").

Now have your child climb in and describe for you and other cabin-bound children the best way to spend time during wintry or rainy days or days when you're not feeling so good. Perhaps he or she can put on a commercial demonstrating the best rainy-day toys to play with.

Required:

Large box (or old sheet and chairs), scissors

Take note: You'll probably gain some great insights into what your kids want to do when they're cabin-bound or sick. And there's another benefit, too: When your kids are *inside* the tube, you don't have to worry about them passing their time *in front of* the real one-eyed monster.

OUT AND ABOUT

Things to Do Instead of . . .

Playing Handheld Games

Alphabet Chase

If you ever see the words *speedy* and *letter* in the same sentence, chances are you aren't talking about the mail. But you might be playing this game.

The object of the game is to see who can reach the end of the alphabet first using letters found on billboards, street signs, store displays, magazine covers, or other printed materials. Players must gather their letters in alphabetical order. That "Appleby's Cafe" sign, for example, offers an *a, b,* and c.

If you're stuck somewhere without access to street signs or billboards, use anything else in view that has letters—posters, pamphlets, and the like.

If you're in traffic, let one team or child use the signs out the right window, while another child or team uses the signs on the left. Or, the youngest kids might get to use any kind of sign, while older kids have to use store signs. From time to time, one team will get stuck while another moves ahead or catches up—there seem to be plenty of *p*'s, but not a lot of *q*'s out there!

The old "I Spy" game can be a sanity saver when your kids are ready to eat but the restaurant is on its own schedule. Here are a few variations that can turn waiting time into instant fun time.

If you're waiting for a table to be cleared, start off a "spy" session by suggesting various objects in the entry area, such as the coat rack, the maître d's microphone, the cash register, plants, and various decorations. Get creative with older kids by offering cryptic clues. For instance, you might say, "I spy something with a mouth that occasionally opens and swallows flat, rectangular green objects and round, shiny disks" (the cash register).

Once you're seated, use objects around the table, such as art on the menu, place mats, napkins, advertising placards, art on the walls, and so on. Don't forget subtle items such as wallpaper, designs in the carpet, and silverware patterns.

Won't everyone be happy when you can call out, "I spy something coming from the kitchen and headed our way"?

Why are your kids rubbing their stomachs and tapping their heads? Because they're speaking in a secret code (they're actually concurring that it's time for an ice-cream break).

You can get in on the action, too, by helping your children devise a code language that can involve words, hand signs, and various types of body language. Start off simple, with a substitute for "yes" and "no." Perhaps patting the head means "yes" and pointing to the nose means "no." Ask a series of yes/no questions, such as, "Is your name Madeline?" "Do you like chocolate?" "Do we live on earth?" Rattle off the questions as quickly as you can, seeing if your kids can keep the hand signals straight.

Next, up the challenge by substituting body language for common words. For instance, pointing to an elbow might mean "table," and waving twice might mean "book." So you might say, "Please pass the green [wave twice] on the [point to elbow]."

See how many substitutions you and your kids can devise. When you're done, you may be able to have a complete conversation without opening your mouths!

Bumble Bee, Bumble Bee

The title of this activity takes its name from the childhood rhyme that always accompanies it in our house: "Bumble bee, bumble bee, I see something that you don't see, and the color of it is . . ."

The person who says the rhyme must choose a single object that's in plain sight. The other players, using only the object's color as a clue, must locate and name the item.

If you have a lot of time to pass, choose an object that's in plain sight but not at first obvious, such as a red hat worn by a model on a billboard. If the wait is short, or if you want a faster-paced game, choose obvious objects, such as a building or a tree.

You can also give your kids clues as to how well they're doing by saying "cold" when they name something far away from the selected object, "warm" when they get closer, and "hot" when they're very close to the right pick.

Because it's based on colors, even very young children can play this game. And you might be surprised at what they notice in the world around them!

Car Talk

If cars could talk, what would they say? You and your child can decide for yourselves next time you're out walking.

Take some time to notice the cars that pass by—pay special attention to the colors, sizes, shapes, and unusual features of the vehicles. Then ask your child to give an impromptu speech in the character of one of the cars. For example, if your child playacts a minivan, he or she might say, "I'm a strong vehicle, and my favorite pastime is to take families for long drives and keep them safe."

After your child finishes the speech, you can ask him or her such questions as: "Can you describe the family that owns you?" "Who is the most interesting passenger you've ever driven?" "What's your favorite route to drive?" and "What's the farthest you've ever traveled?" (Your child answers all questions in character.)

Your child can also playact such vehicles as bicycles, trucks, vans, airplanes, or any other modes of transportation you see in your travels. Now, what do you suppose that skateboard is thinking?

Here's an activity that will turn any waiting room into an amusement park for the mind. And you won't have to turn it upside down either!

The idea is to have your child focus on some aspect of the room and then close his or her eyes. You then alter something and see if he or she can figure out what's different. For example, let's say that the waiting room has a stack of magazines on a coffee table, and the top magazine happens to have a red cover. Have your child look in the vicinity of the table, then, while his or her eyes are closed, place a different magazine on top.

You can also rearrange coats on a coatrack, place a brochure backwards in a rack, or conduct other little bits of chicanery that won't cause anyone extra work to tidy up (you might suggest a rule that the room changer puts everything back the way it was after a round of guessing has taken place).

Say, do you suppose there's always been a mitten hanging on that ficus tree by the window?

Changing Scenery

What will the street that you and your child are walking along look like three months from now? In six months? How about in ten months? Just ask your child, and you're likely to get a pretty interesting picture.

Name a season other than the current one, and ask your child to describe what he or she would be seeing along your walking path if it were that time of year. Say you want it to be wintertime. Your child might then tell you that there's just been a blizzard that's buried the street under six feet of snow, and you can barely see the tops of the chimneys. Or perhaps there's a snowman under construction in the yard next door, and if you look carefully, you can see a whole snow family lined up behind him!

Your child might also point out decorations that people have put up in anticipation of a holiday during the season you specify. Hmm, how many make-believe Fourth of July flags can your child count in March?

If you have a handful of coins and a tabletop nearby, then you have all you need to turn waiting time into a series of exciting coin games.

Drop your coins on the table, and ask your child to sort them according to type: quarters, dimes, nickels, and pennies. Then see whether your sorter can group together various coin combinations, such as two quarters and four dimes, six pennies and two nickels, three dimes and one penny, and so on.

You can also suggest that your child make coin patterns by lining up the coins in whichever order you specify—say, two pennies and a dime, followed by one penny and a dime—across the table. See whether your child can guess how many coins, or how many pattern sets, it will take to make a line from edge to edge. As your child gets better at the pattern game, increase the challenge by suggesting more complex patterns.

We've noticed another pattern; the more simple coin games you play, the faster the waiting time seems to fly!

Crazy Street Signs

Stuck in traffic? Pass some time by turning work and road signs into wacky, funny messages.

To make the game challenging for all, suggest a couple of simple ground rules (after that, anything goes!). First off, a player can only change one word on the sign. Second, the word that gets changed must begin with the same letter as the word that takes its place. As an alternative, you might try substituting words that rhyme for the words in the sign.

Take the "Men at Work" sign over that manhole. That sign could become "Martians at Work." Or, that "No Trespassing" sign can become "No Trampolining" or "No Trapeze Acts." And that bothersome "No Parking Zone"? Why not make it the "No Barking Zone"!

Excuse me, Bowser—can't you read the sign?

It's a clock, a can opener, a telephone, and a hair dryer—all in one! Here's an opportunity to invent the ultimate combo machine and pass some waiting time.

Ask your child to imagine a single machine that could do everything you need to get done in a day, from the morning events to lights-out at night. The machine would have to be able to help with waking up, preparing breakfast, cleaning up dishes, whisking kids off to school and parents to work, meetings, errands, or back home again, picking kids up in the afternoon, preparing and serving meals at dinner time, getting everyone ready for bed, and finally making sure the house is closed up for the evening.

Have your child describe or draw the resulting contraption. Maybe it's a robot with wheels and seats. Or perhaps it's more like a car with mechanical arms. Whatever it is, we could sure use one at our house, so have your child send us a sketch immediately!

Fender-to-Fender Football

Here's a football activity that doesn't require any special equipment—or a ref, because there aren't any penalties.

Kick off the game by choosing offense or defense. The offensive player selects a color and tells it to the defensive player. To stop the offense from making a touchdown, the defensive player must find four objects (one per down) that are the same color as that named by the offense.

If the defense can't find the right-colored objects in a specified time, or before a specified distance is covered, the offense scores a first down. The offense gets to choose another color and attempts to make another first down. Two or three first downs take you all the way down the field for a touchdown, at which point offense and defense switch goals. If the defense does find four objects, the player becomes the offense. To keep the game going, each player must choose a different (primary) color each time.

All right, sports fans, block the boredom—get off the sidelines and into the game!

Here's an imagination game that will keep everyone's mind humming along while their food is simmering away in the restaurant kitchen.

The object is to see who can concoct a meal from the menu that would be entirely one color (or almost all one color). For instance, a green meal might consist of split pea soup, a salad with lettuce and avocados, a side order of green beans, and pistachio ice cream. A red meal might be tomato soup, tomato noodles with spaghetti sauce, red cabbage coleslaw, cranberry juice, and strawberry ice cream. Then try to come up with a white, purple, yellow, or orange meal.

First see who can make the meal as balanced and appealing as possible. Then suggest that everyone tries to make the zaniest meal possible, with odd concoctions and "exotic" foods.

Hmm, mashed potatoes covered with pink lemonade certainly would give you a pink vegetable. But you'll probably want to take a pass on it when it comes to ordering!

Fresh Off the Press

If your local supermarket offers weekly circulars, then you and your child have the makings of some appealing waiting games. Have your child pick up a circular at the store (or bring one from home), and ask him or her to find: all the fruits, the red items, the foods with seeds, the vegetables with leaves, and so on.

Your older child can use the circular to practice some supermarket math. You might ask, "What would it cost if we bought three jars of peanut butter and four cans of tuna?" Or, "If we had ten dollars, would we have enough money to buy a package of chicken, a bunch of broccoli, and two boxes of macaroni?"

Your kids can also match sale items from the circular with the real things on the shelves. If coupons are available, your children can be responsible for pointing them out to you. That may result in some unexpected purchases, though; you probably didn't expect to buy two jars of anchovy paste and get one free!

Here's a fun word game that uses the names of places. It doesn't take more than a good memory for geography, but watch out—the longer you play, the harder it gets.

The rules are simple. One player starts by saying the name of a place—town, city, state, country, and so on. Each player in turn has to think of a place name that begins with the *last* letter of the previous place.

For example, the first player might start with New York. Player two could say Kansas, leaving player three with an S. The game could then go on with Saskatoon, Nepal, Louisiana, Amarillo, Oregon, New Hampshire, Ethiopia, Arkansas, Santa Barbara, Anchorage—until a player gets stumped!

If your kids have fun with this game, you can try it with other categories as well, like foods or people's names. No doubt, the waiting time will be over long before you've run out of words to use!

"This is the Smith's house. Please leave a message and we'll call you back later." Oh, yawn. Your kids can no doubt improve on that answering machine message and have some waiting time fun in the process. Let them devise some messages about:

Famous people. How about, "Hi, this is Ben Franklin, I'm out flying a kite in a lightning storm and can't talk to you now. Catch you later. Ahhh-hhhhhhh!"

Zany Situations. Perhaps, "Hi. This is George, I can't talk now because I'm hanging upside down from the tree in the backyard doing my home-work!"

Silly Voice-Mail Menus. Take revenge on today's awful voice-mail systems with something like: "Hi. Press one if you want to leave a message, then choose from the following thirty-two choices, spin twice, touch your ear, hang up, and send us a letter!"

Leave any waiting grumpies at the beep!

Hey, is that a real flamingo over in the corner, or is it just your child playacting?

Choose a creature (mammal, fish, bird, or insect), and have your child improvise a member of the species. He or she acts out the creature physically (by hopping, leaping, flapping his or her "wings," standing on one leg, and so on). Your job is to guess which type of creature your child is playacting.

If you need additional clues, your child might turn his or her creature into a talking animal, fish, bird, or insect, and offer clues. A flying fish, for example, might say something like, "I mainly live in the water, but I enjoy taking to the air now and then." A caterpillar might say, "It takes a long time for me to tie my eighteen shoes . . . but after sleeping for a while, I'll wake up and only have to worry about six—when I'm not flying, that is."

Once you guess your child's creature, you can improvise another and see if your child can figure out what you are. Don't worry about anyone staring—it's all in a day's wait!

Hand Signals

Why should people who drive cars using hand signals have all the fun? Your child can use a similar body language to direct you while you're walking to an appointment or event.

Have your child develop hand signals that designate a left turn, right turn, straight ahead motion, or reverse motion. Then let your child direct you using those signs to let you and other followers know what to do (of course, when your child reaches the end of a street or the corner, he or she should adhere to your family's standard safety rules and let you take over the position of leader as necessary).

Enhance the language by developing additional signals. For example, raising the left arm twice might mean "hop on your right foot until further notice," making the victory sign with the left hand might mean "take baby steps," and raising both arms at once might mean "step over cracks in the sidewalk."

See how long you can follow your child's hand signals before you get confused!

How would you like to tour a museum while you're waiting? Well, get ready to have your child take you on an instant tour of the Anywhere Museum!

Your child can lead you on a guided walk through an office building, the subway stop, or wherever you happen to be, pointing out all of the original features (such as the stairway that was handcarved by the first carpenter in Neanderthal times), the newer additions (like the drinking fountain that was installed just after the discovery of metal), interesting furnishings (such as the chair that George Washington sat in when he came to town), and so on.

In addition, your tour guide/child can tell you about previous occupants of the house or building: their names, occupations, favorite pastimes, any additions or modifications that they made to the structure. Be sure to ask lots of questions of your guide—everything in the museum probably has a fascinating hidden history!

How Many Words?

What's in a restaurant's name and a restaurant's menu? Good waiting games for your kids, probably.

First try seeing how many distinct words your children can discover using the letters in the name of the restaurant you're patronizing. If the establishment is called something like "The Grand Old New England Clam Chowder House," it'll be easy for everyone to come up with a slew of words. If it's "Al's," you might want to try using words from the menu. For instance, how many words can people find in sandwich entrees such as "Hamburger Deluxe" or "Grilled Cheese Special"? Make sure each player gets a chance to pick a section of the menu for the next round of the game.

As a variation, each player tries to find his or her name in the fewest number of words on the menu. To make the name "Steve," for example, you'd need a "Side Order," (an s and two e's), a "Taco" (for the t), and "Virginia Ham" (for the v).

As these games will show, it pays to go to restaurants with varied menus!

It's bad enough when your child has to sit in a doctor's waiting room for a long time; it's worse when he or she dreads the appointment. Here's a way to make the time pass more quickly and dispel some anxiety.

Do a little role reversal, and have your child ask you various questions, such as, "So what's the doctor going to do today?" You then talk about what's likely to happen and ask your child what you can do to be brave.

You can also provide some comic relief by offering silly scenarios, such as, "Well, I'm a bit nervous, because the doctor is going to put Oreo cookies between my toes and stinky cheese on my head." Your child can then assure you that there's nothing to worry about; the cheese aroma won't last more than a month, and the cookie filling will keep your feet warm during winter!

When it's time to see the doctor, your child will be giggling with a host of remedies to share with the medical staff!

Howdy, Neighbor

Here's a quick quiz to challenge your children's knowledge of U.S. geography. In the list below, the first state in each set shares a border with some or all of the other states in that set. Can your kids tell you which ones share borders? (Correct answers are in *italics*.)

Wyoming shares a border with—
    North Dakota? *South Dakota?*
Maryland shares a border with–
    Delaware? West Virginia? New Jersey?
New Mexico shares a border with—
    Oklahoma? Nevada?
Vermont shares a border with—
    Maine? *New Hampshire? Massachusetts?*
Kansas shares a border with–
    Arkansas? *Colorado? Missouri?*
South Carolina shares a border with—
    Florida? *Georgia?* Tennessee?
California shares a border with—
    Idaho? *Arizona? Nevada?*
Wisconsin shares a border with—
    Michigan? Iowa? Indiana?
Texas shares a border with—
    New Mexico? Oklahoma? Arkansas? Louisiana?

And for a bonus, ask: The Mississippi River runs along or through ten states—What are they? (*Minnesota, Wisconsin, Iowa, Illinois, Missouri, Kentucky, Tennessee, Arkansas, Mississippi, and Louisiana*)

Making music is one of the best ways we have of passing the time. Here are some suggestions for using singing to create your own waiting games.

If you have young kids with you, take turns humming a song and see who can guess the name. Stick to old favorites like *This Old Man*. During special holidays, try humming seasonal tunes.

Another musical game—"song charades"—doesn't involve humming or singing at all. One player silently acts out a song, while the others try to guess what it is. An alternative way to guess is to hum the tune instead of saying the answer.

Other variations include clapping out a tune, and humming a song in a monotone.

Finally, do a "Johnny-One-Note" hum-along. To play, choose a song. Each person hums a single note in turn, around and around until the whole song is sung. Kind of makes you feel like you're part of a human pipe organ!

Release your child's imagination with this story activity that gives a voice to the inanimate objects all around you. Take the old bank there on the corner. What's it thinking? What does it sound like? If it could talk, what would it say?

In this activity, you and your child take turns speaking like the cars, trucks, buildings, signs, and structures that surround your car during rush hour. If your child doesn't know how to begin, start with something like the Walk/Don't Walk light at the intersection. "Please be careful, says the light," you might say. "Look both ways. Hurry across now."

Movie theaters are always great conversationalists. "Come right on in," they say from their big dark doorways "It's a really great show I've got playing here."

The vehicles on the road in front and to the side can provide a lot of fun as they jostle for position. "Excuse me," says the taxi cab, pushing its nose in front of the bus. "Well, I never," exclaims the bus. "The nerve!"

Wouldn't you like to interview an astronaut while you're waiting? Well, designate your child an intergalactic traveler, and see whether you can snag a one-on-one conversation.

Your child role-plays a space traveler who has just returned from an intergalactic mission. As the first reporter on the scene, your job is to get all the information you can about the expedition. Ask such questions as: Which planets did you visit? How long did you spend in outer space? What did you do to pass the time while you were traveling? Did you meet any life forms on other planets? What did you find on the most interesting planets you visited? How did the moons you visited differ from our moon? What did you eat while you were traveling?

Perhaps your child brought some surprises back to earth, like some other-worldly rocks, seashells, instant pictures, plants—or even a new alien buddy. See whether you can be the first earthling reporter to speak with an extraterrestrial once you've finished interviewing your child!

What if your children were suddenly *heard but not seen* because they were invisible? Ask how they would:

Enjoy the perks of being invisible. What would your kids do that visible kids can't? Would they still take baths? Would they get sneak previews of museum exhibits off-limits to the public?

Conduct themselves in public. What pleasant mischief would they get themselves into? Perhaps they'd tickle people waiting in line in stores or adjust people's hats as they rode a bus.

Get people's attention politely and without scaring them. If your kids sat down, how would they let people know "this seat is taken"? How would your children let teachers know when they wanted to be called on? How would your kids greet their friends and initiate conversations?

Once your kids have thought about what it might be like to be invisible, pose this question: If you could be heard but not seen, would you?

Most pediatricians' offices have lots of pictures of children—photographs of patients, or drawings and photos in brochures, pamphlets, magazines, posters, and paintings. Here's how you can use them while you wait your turn for your child to be seen.

First, see how many pictures of kids your child can find. If your child hasn't developed counting skills yet, he or she can simply point to each picture and you can keep a running tally. Next, have your junior sleuth track down all the pictures of babies, all those of girls, all the boys, and so on.

If the wait is really dragging on, you can suggest various "specialty" hunts, such as all the girls with brown hair, all the boys with glasses, everyone wearing something red, everyone smiling, and so on.

If you have more than one child with you, each can be assigned a certain type of picture to find. You can up the challenge by limiting the time of the picture hunt.

Hey, there's a fun-looking family—it's yours!

How well do your kids know U.S. geography? Put them to the test by having them try to name all fifty states! Then see if your children can tell you the postal abbreviation for each state—or tell your kids an abbreviation and have them identify the state.

Alabama	AL	Montana	MT
Alaska	AK	Nebraska	NE
Arizona	AZ	Nevada	NV
Arkansas	AR	New Hampshire	NH
California	CA	New Jersey	NJ
Colorado	CO	New Mexico	NM
Connecticut	CT	New York	NY
Delaware	DE	North Carolina	NC
Florida	FL	North Dakota	ND
Georgia	GA	Ohio	OH
Hawaii	HI	Oklahoma	OK
Idaho	ID	Oregon	OR
Illinois	IL	Pennsylvania	PA
Indiana	IN	Rhode Island	RI
Iowa	IA	South Carolina	SC
Kansas	KS	South Dakota	SD
Kentucky	KY	Tennessee	TN
Louisiana	LA	Texas	TX
Maine	ME	Utah	UT
Maryland	MD	Vermont	VT
Massachusetts	MA	Virginia	VA
Michigan	MI	Washington	WA
Minnesota	MN	West Virginia	WV
Mississippi	MS	Wisconsin	WI
Missouri	MO	Wyoming	WY

Bonus question: Who knows their 9-digit zip code? Beats us!

OUT AND ABOUT

Need a fast, short, easy game to play with your kids? This game turns any wait into a red-letter day.

Start the game by naming a letter. Then, on the simplest level, your child must list as many things beginning with that letter as he or she can see in the immediate surroundings. If more than one child is playing, each child should take a turn naming an object. To increase the challenge, ask your kids to name objects that end with the letter you have selected.

A variation involves entire words. To play, name the word: "hat," for example. The key here is to keep the words simple—no more than three or four letters. Your kids must find three objects, each of which contains one letter of the selected word—like "helicopter," "animal," and "lamp-post." Modify the difficulty level by letting kids use any letters in the objects they see, or by restricting them to beginning or ending letters.

Here's a chance for any child to earn his or her letter jacket while you wait!

Line Math

When are we going to get our tickets?

When is it our turn? You can offer some precise answers after you and your older children do
some "line math."

Try computing how fast the line is moving by
picking something on the floor or ground that
will serve as a marker, then timing how long it
takes to move, say, three feet (approximate as best
you can). Take a best guess as to how far you are
from the beginning of the line, and have your
child calculate how long it will take to "get there."
(Having a pad and pencil will help.)

Another way to compute the time is observe
how many people are admitted, purchase tickets,
or whatever every minute, then count how many
people are in front of you. Some quick math will
give you a precise answer.

What to do if the waiting seems awfully long?
Why, see who can convert the waiting times into
fractions of a day, week, month, year, decade, or
century. See, it's not such a long time after all.

Isn't it about time you learned to pick the fastest checkout line at the supermarket? Perhaps, with the help of your child's keen eye for detail, you can.

Ask your child to predict which line will move the fastest and explain why. Perhaps the express line, which is the longest, is still the best bet because customers have the fewest purchases. Or maybe the cashier in aisle six has the shortest line, and is working at warp speed, so her line is sure to move the most quickly. You might choose the line your child recommends, or pick another as a "control" and see whether or not your child was right.

Your child can also officiate at a "Line Olympics." While you're waiting in line, your child can keep an eye on two different lines (the ones on either side of yours), and predict which line will move the fastest. The easiest method is to keep an eye on customers in specific positions (say, the fourth person in line), and see which ones pay for their purchases first.

Hmm, do you think that couple with four grocery carts will ever get through the line?

Hey, what's that lion doing here in the doctor's waiting room? Probably waiting to have a thorn pulled out of his paw.

As you wait your turn with the doctor, ask your child to imagine how he or she would treat a lion (or any other animal) with an injured paw. Young children can even demonstrate proper medical techniques with a stuffed animal, if the waiting room has one, or by using your hand (perhaps thorn removal requires applying pressure in just the right way—with a strong chin). Be sure to have your child offer the lion words of consolation and advice on how to be brave.

Suggest other scenarios as well, such as an elephant whose trunk became clogged with peanuts (the doctor always keeps a special vacuum attachment for such problems), or the hippo whose mouth got stuck open when she yawned too wide (tickling behind the ears is a proven method for such problems!).

Now then, how will your child treat that poor octopus with the sucker that seems permanently stuck to a Ping-Pong ball?

So your kids are tired of waiting and are getting bored? Just have them look around at all the exciting things that have interesting histories.

Take that doorknob over there. Who invented it? And when? Ask your resident expert questions like "Why were doorknobs necessary?" "What did people do without them?" "What was the person's name who came up with the idea?" "What kind of commotion did the invention make in the town where the inventor lived?" and so on.

You can also turn the session into a role-play activity, during which you take the position of a naysayer. "What? Impossible! Doorknobs will forever alter the shape of human hands!!!"

You can play this game with just about anything from concrete and glass to shoelaces and ballpoint pens. All of the things you take for granted are grist for the expert's mill. For that matter, what is the story behind the old gristmill?

More Coin Games

What are coins really worth these days?

Ask your child to answer that question without looking at the money, and you'll find the time flying.

Have your child close his or her eyes, then place a quarter, dime, nickel, and penny in his or her hand. See if he or she can identify which is which. If your child can't feel the difference between the coins, give him or her an "eyes open study period" first. For hotshots, try including a "ringer," say two pennies and no dime—will your child recognize the trick or convince him- or herself that one of the pennies is actually a dime?

As a variation, see if your child can find a dollar's worth of coins, five coins that add up to forty-five cents, or five coins that add up to nine cents—all with his or her eyes closed.

Hey, how about this one: How many quarters will it take to pay the parking ticket that the meter maid is about to tuck under your windshield?

Of course, every child *knows* his or her birthday. But can your kids *find* the date by looking at the numbers on signs, clocks, magazines, and so on?

Have your children translate their birthdays into numerical form, including the month, day, and year (for example, 6–10–87 and 3–31–90). Then see if they can find those numbers, in sequence, as you walk or ride (check house, road, and exit numbers), or while you sit (look at magazines and newspapers, or a calendar).

Once your kids find their birthdays, see whether they can find yours and other family members'. Then have them look for other familiar dates, with or without years, such as 7–4 (Independence Day), 2–14 (Valentine's Day), and so on. Your child can also seek other important, non-date numbers, such as addresses, ages, and so on.

Can anybody find your telephone number—all in one source?

Mosts and Leasts

When you're waiting, do you feel like you've blended into a homogeneous line, a veritable mass of humanity? With a little observation on your child's part, the line will suddenly take on a unique life of its own.

Have your child look at the people in line (without pointing) and observe the following (noting the most and least common): clothing colors in general (clothing, purses, bags), as well as the colors of specific apparel, such as hats, coats, pants, etc.; hair color—men, women, and everyone in line; clothing styles (for example, how many people have shorts, long pants, sweatshirts, jackets); how many wear glasses; how many are with children; and so on.

You can add another dimension to the game by guessing beforehand which will be the most prevalent color hat, mode of dress, etc. Or, based on the calculations, try to predict the look of the next people to join the line.

So, are you really just another face in the line, or does your family represent a new line of trendsetters?

It's said that climbing Mount Everest or the Matterhorn is one of the most daring feats that a mountaineer can undertake. The next time you and your kids are waiting, go on a climbing expedition of your own—using your imagination.

Pick a tall building and imagine you're going to scale its heights. If you're inside, pretend that you're very tiny and you have to scale the lamp, or table, or chair.

Before you start climbing, figure out what kind of tools you'll need to make the climb. You will need some rope, backpacks for supplies, a harness for safety, and maybe some special tools like grappling hooks and rubber-soled shoes.

Then, as you embark on your imaginary climb, figure out how your expedition team will conquer each obstacle. What if you come to a huge window? Did you remember to bring suction cups? You can even get comical with your supplies: Bang on the window until the building custodian brings you a toilet plunger, then tie the plunger to your leg and use it to traverse the glass.

By the time you get back to the ground, your wait will be over.

My Strangest Case

Here's a great way to pass some time in a waiting room—and, if it happens to be the waiting room of the doctor or dentist, defuse a little anxiety.

Take turns imagining that you're the doctor or dentist, and that you're relaying the strangest case of the day, like the person who swallowed a tuba and every time he exhaled he sounded like a foghorn. Perhaps as a dentist, you've seen a young fellow who brushed his teeth with white glue by mistake and couldn't open his mouth.

This activity works well in *any* waiting room situation. Perhaps you're waiting for an oil change or car repair; you and your child can take turns pretending you're the mechanic and describing oddities such as the person who locked an egg-salad sandwich in the glove compartment and lost the key.

You can also play this game by describing the problem and seeing if your child can guess what happened. You're bound to get some interesting answers. Perhaps the person who swallowed the tuba got a new job with the Coast Guard!

When you have kids, most of the places you go to eat don't make you wait long. Just shout into the clown's mouth and stop at the window. If you set your gastronomic sights higher, hold on to the menus after placing your order. Those folded papers are a ready-made word game for your kids.

Each player in the game takes a turn with the menu. Starting with the appetizers, the player uses the first selection to make a new word. "Crab Cakes," for example, can be used to make the word "brake."

The next player uses the same selection as his or her starting word. Play continues around the table, until one person can't form an original word. That player gets one mark (you can keep score by handing out sugar packets), then selects the next item on the menu.

The game can continue until your meal is served. The player with the fewest packets wins— besides, they always say that less sugar is better!

What if the whole world were one big nation, and individual countries no longer existed? Ask your kids how we would:

Govern all the people in the world.   Would we have government by one big world tribunal, or would we have a host of smaller tribunals? How would we make sure that everyone had fair representation?

Speak.   Would everybody speak the same language? How would we decide which language was the official worldwide tongue? Would people be allowed to speak whichever language they wanted to? How could we steer them toward the official language?

Get along.   How could people who have different customs, foods, clothing, religions, and even holidays learn to live in the same country with one another? Would we find it easier or more difficult to get along with each other?

Once your kids have thought about what it might be like to live in a world without individual countries, pose this question: Would you like to live in a world composed of just one country?

Here's a doodling activity that you and your child can go into with your eyes closed—as long as you plan to have some belly laughs when you're through.

Make sure each of you has a piece of drawing paper and a pencil. One person calls out an object (a clock, car, building, person, and so on). The other then tries to draw the object while keeping his or her eyes closed. When the drawing is finished, both of you look at the picture, and chuckle at the results.

For extra fun, suggest that your child draw a geometric shape (eyes open). Then suggest that he or she turn the shape into an object with his or her eyes closed. For example, your child might start off drawing a rectangle and wind up adding three circles in a column inside. What is it? A traffic light perhaps. Or perhaps it's a front view of an electronic instrument (just add numbers and pointers to the circles). With this game, the truth only lies in the eyes of the beholder!

It takes a good orator to make an excellent speech on an important topic. But it takes a great orator—like your child—to give an extemporaneous speech about practically anything!

When you have some extra time, and your child is in a talkative mood, point to any object. Then have your child make a speech about it. You might specify a time limit—say, three minutes—during which your speech maker can talk about the object's history, who invented it, what earlier versions looked like, how it was first used, how it's used today, how it might be improved or adapted in the future, and so on.

For a real challenge, point to an obscure object such as the eraser at the end of a pencil, the plastic ends on a shoelace, or the T-shaped piece of plastic that holds a tag on a new item of clothing. See whether your child can make a full-length speech on the subject. Perhaps he or she can even tell you what the tagholder is really called!

On the Other Hand . . .

:::::::::::::::::
::::::
:::: **231**
::::::
:::::::::::::::::

What if everyone in the world drew with the "wrong" hand (the opposite of the hand he or she wrote with)? We'd have some very funny drawings, that's for sure!

Draw a simple picture and ask your child to copy it on another piece of paper. The hitch, of course, is that your child has to make the copy using his or her non-dominant hand (ambidextrous kids might want to try the exercise with either hand, but with their eyes closed). To really challenge your child's "wrong-hand" dexterity, add more complicated shapes and patterns to the original drawing, and then see whether your child can copy them, too. Your child can then try the drawing again, but this time, with his or her dominant hand. Isn't it amazing what a difference a hand makes?

And speaking of a-mazing, why not draw a maze on a blank sheet of paper? Using his or her non-dominant hand, your child then tries to draw a line through the maze without letting the pencil touch any of the walls. Now, give your child a hand for a great effort!

What if your children were just one inch tall? Ask how they would:

Navigate stairs. Perhaps they would lower a string from a bannister and slide down it, or invent an elevator made from a paper cup and a string.

Eat. Since pots, pans, dishes, cups, and silverware would be too large, what would your kids eat and drink from instead? What foods would they eat, and what size would the portions be? Perhaps a single corn flake would constitute a whole meal!

Find clothing that fit. Since your kids' old clothes would be far too large, they would have to make a new wardrobe. What would *they* use for materials? Perhaps a cloth napkin would provide enough material to make a whole closetful of outfits.

Once your kids have thought about what life in miniature would be like, pose the following question: If it were possible to be an inch tall for a while, would you want to try it? Why or why not?

How big is the waiting room, restaurant lobby, or movie theater lobby? You'll find out (well, sort of) after your child does some custom measurements.

First have your child pace out the room, or whatever you'd like measured. Then take a guess (unless you happen to have a ruler handy—the receptionist might) as to the length of each pace, in inches. See if your child can figure out the total number of inches. If he or she can divide by twelve, you'll know the answer in feet.

A younger kid will simply enjoy reporting that the room is thirty-five big steps long, or that a hallway is twenty-two giant steps. You can record the numbers on a notepad to make the entries "official."

Your younger child will also probably enjoy making a zany equivalency. For example, one big stride might be a "dinostep," and a baby step might be a "duck hop." So he or she might report that a room is ten dinosteps and one duck hop long.

Keep good notes—you might have some surprising news for the architect who designed the building!

Point Counterpoint

It's no fun debating a child about when it's time to go to bed or what to eat. But debates about other topics can be a great way to pass the time. Try debating these topics with your younger child:

1. What's the best ice-cream flavor?
2. Which is the best dinosaur?
3. What's the most unusual animal?
4. What is the best time of the day?
5. What is the best age to be?
6. What's the most fun thing for a kid to do?
7. What's the most fun thing for a grown-up to do?
8. Are baths important?
9. Are table manners important?
10. Is it better to be a big brother/sister or a little brother/sister?

Don't stop here, though—try this one: What's the most fun thing to do when you have to wait?

What's in a restaurant's name? Just about everything you and your child need to know about the eating establishment—especially if *you* choose its name!

While you're waiting to be served, ask your child to suggest new names for the restaurant. The moniker can express your child's first impression of the restaurant (for example, "The Pizza Palace of Great Potential"). Or, if the restaurant is a tried-and-true family favorite, the name might be based on the types of foods that the restaurant offers ("The Something-for-Everyone Shop"), how often you eat there ("Once-a-Weekend Eatery"), the way you discovered it ("Grandma's Find of the Year"), what the furniture looks like ("Green Chair Cafe"), and so on.

Your child might also name the restaurant according to the "best" meal that's served there ("The Best House of Hamburgers"). If you have more than one young diner, make sure *each* child gets a chance to name the restaurant. Who knows—maybe the owners will take a hint from your family!

What if it were possible to make anti-gravity machines? Ask your kids how the machines would:

Change the world. Would it be necessary to have elevators or escalators? Or could people simply float up inside tubes to whatever floor they wanted to go and grab hold of "floor handles?" How about anti-gravity boots; perhaps runners could simply "anti-grav" hop over obstacles.

Lead to new forms of entertainment. Maybe we'd see the first "Anti-Gravity Arena," where people bounced off foam ceilings, kind of like reverse bungee jumping. What other kinds of games and thrills can your kids envision?

Avoid misuse of the devices. How could we prevent mishaps, such as people floating off into space, or anti-gravity machines accidentally turning on and disrupting a whole building or community?

Once your kids have thought about these issues, pose this question: Would you want an anti-gravity machine, if somebody offered to build one for you?

Everybody is born a poet—and here's a way to show it. You can play this game with one child or with a group of kids. To start, the first player announces a word. The next player has five seconds (you can allow more time) to say a word that rhymes with the original word. For example, if the first player says "car," the next player says something like "tar."

No repeats are allowed; each word has to be original. If you're playing with just one child, take turns thinking of words. If a group is playing, a player is eliminated if he or she can't think of a matching word. The last player left gets to pick the next word.

If you're playing with older kids, you can use words that are more difficult to find matches for: "boulder," "shoulder," and "older," for example. For very young children, stick with simple three- and four-letter words.

And when your kids stumble onto a word like "orange" or "purple," you'll just have to smile and make the best of it.

Shoes Game

Everybody waiting in line generally has one thing in common. Well, two actually. Shoes! Your kids can have a great time passing the time cataloging all the different shoe types they see.

Start off by seeing how many different types of shoes your child can identify, such as high heels, sneakers, saddle shoes, loafers, sandals, boots, or whatever you're likely to see in your part of the country (make sure your kids stay within sight). Then ask for a count of each type and a determination of which is the most and least common.

To increase the challenge, have your shoe sleuths try to find shoe types of certain colors or locate laces or socks of certain colors or styles. You might for instance say, "Let's find a pair of brown sandals." "Who can spot a blue pair of running shoes and white socks?" or "The first person to locate the shoe gets to make the next 'find it' request."

For the supreme challenge, see if your kids can find the exact pairs of shoes they are wearing—complete with grass stains and chocolate ice-cream drips!

Here's a quick way to put your observational powers to work—and watch the time fly!

To get the game going, start with the shortest object in your surroundings. It doesn't have to be small—something close to the ground will do. You can even start with the ground if you want, or with the sidewalk or street. The next player then picks an object that's a little taller. All of the players continue taking turns until one player can't find an object taller than the last one selected.

Think of it as that old game kids play with a baseball bat, putting one hand over the next until they reach the top of the handle. As you play, you may need to set up some rules; don't let kids jump from the street to the tallest skyscraper in a single turn.

If you're playing with your kids, and they manage to work all the way up to the tallest building downtown—well, you might have to keep a lookout for a helicopter or a plane flying by.

Sign Jumbles

The Word Jumbles in the newspaper are one of our favorite ways to pass the time. But you don't need a newspaper to play word games—any sign will do.

To play, just turn your attention to the billboards, store displays, and traffic signs all around you. This is a great way to pass the time while waiting on a bus, or while stopped in traffic.

The object of the game is to see how many words can be made out of the letters on the sign. That stop sign on the corner, for example, contains the word *spot.* The marquee outside of the cafe holds the word *face.*

When you and your child play together, keep using the same sign until it stumps one of you. The last player to get a word from the sign is the winner.

If you're playing in the car, and you're stopped at a traffic light, keep going until the light turns green—but you'll have to think fast! Just how many words can you get out of that "Pedestrian Crossing" sign, anyway?

Here's a great way to stretch the imagination and shrink the waiting time. While in the doctor's or dentist's office, or while waiting for a haircut, pick up a magazine from one of the tables. Your best choice is a magazine suitable for kids, but any magazine will do.

The first player closes his or her eyes, opens the magazine, and puts a finger on the page. Then, after opening his or her eyes, the player must read the word under his or her finger and make up an opening sentence using that word. For example, if you point to the word *bank,* you could start a story with: "One morning, Marvin the Mongoose decided to pay a visit to the bank."

The next player does the same thing, but his or her sentence must continue the story. See what kind of story unfolds—it might just be Pulitzer Prize–winning stuff!

Songmaker

Kids love to sing, but you don't need to carry around a songbook to keep them in tune. Some of the favorite songs in our family are the ones we made up ourselves.

Kids as young as five can help create songs if you borrow the tune from a song they already know. Once you have a tune, suggest a theme that your child is interested in

A theme that works great for us is dinosaurs. We have songs about a Stegosaurus sleeping in the bed, a duckbill hiding in the tree, even a tyrannosaurus who is growling in the yard. Whatever your kids are interested in, from trains to dolls, can be used to make the song.

Older kids will enjoy trying out different lyrics and rhymes to get the song just right. Take turns making up verses and working with the other singers to build an entire song.

When you get home, you can write your songs down and illustrate them. If you have a tape player, record the finished songs—then you can play them in the car while traveling (and you won't forget the tune).

Are you and your child hearing double? It's likely that you will be, once you've discovered these soundalike word games.

First you'll want to explain to your child that homonyms are two words that sound the same and are spelled the same, but mean two different things. Offer your child some examples of homonyms, such as the words *bat* (a flying rodent) and *bat* (as in baseball bat). Then ask your child to come up with other examples of homonyms.

Still waiting? Then tell your child that homophones are words that sound the same but are spelled differently. Provide some examples, such as *know* and *no,* and *whole* and *hole,* and see whether your child can offer some additional homophones.

Finally, if you have more time to pass, you can ask your child to invent some "sillophones." Sillophones are related to homophones, except that the second soundalike word doesn't exist until your child creates it. For example, "kid" and "cid" are sillophones; of course, a cid is an expert at inventing sillophones!

Every community has its own set of sounds. Next time you and your child are walking to an appointment or event, see how many sounds you can identify.

Listen quietly for a while, then ask your child to name some sounds and the soundmakers. For example, your child might hear engines humming in cars, wind rustling through trees, construction equipment working on building sites, and so on. Ask your child to describe each sound in detail, as well as its source.

As a variation, your child can describe a sound and challenge you to identify the object making it. How long will it take you to figure out that the "ocean's roar" is really the wind whistling through the leaves?

You and your child can also take turns imitating the sounds that you hear. Bet you didn't know that you had such a great bulldozer in you!

As this activity will show, if you have a pencil and a paper napkin or place mat (or a note pad), you're all set to pass some time until the waiter or waitress takes your order or brings your food to the table. (It's actually a take-off on the old "hangman" game, but in honor of the meal-time spirit, we've done away with the unpleasant metaphor.)

Find a word on a menu, a sign on the wall, a decoration, advertising placard, and so on. Then draw enough blank lines for each letter. The players then take turns offering letters. Write down each correct letter in its proper place. For each incorrect guess, you write down a letter, in sequence, of the restaurant's name.

The object is for your kids to figure out the word before you spell out the entire name of the restaurant. (Note: If the name is exceptionally short or long, you might want to offer another name or word that you'll use to record incorrect guesses.) The person who finishes the round gets to choose the next word, and the game continues—until the food arrives, at which point EVERYONE is a winner!

We all know that every walk to an appointment or event begins with a single step. But did you know that the trick to playing a great walking game is to count how many steps you and your child actually take?

Pick a landmark that you'll pass—say, the fire hydrant or the stop sign a couple of blocks away. Then you and your child guess how many steps it will take you to reach that spot (each walker guesses the number of his or her own strides). See which of you comes closest to the number you guessed; the winner gets to choose the rules of the next game. Perhaps your new objective is to guess how many hops it will take to reach the oak tree, how many skips it will take to get to the bank, and so on.

As a variation, you and your child can pick a number of steps and see whether you can reach a predetermined destination—say, a traffic light—in that number of strides. OK, do you think that you and your child can take one hundred steps down a single block?

What . . . no paper or crayons? Try these quick and easy games to keep your kids occupied until you're served.

Tic-Tac-Toe.   Arrange the silverware in a tic-tac-toe grid, crossing two forks over two knives. Then use sugar or sweetener packets as the "Xs" and "Os." If the table isn't stocked with two different types of packets, players can use one side of the packets to represent the "Xs" and the other side for the "Os."

Edge Game.   Two players on opposite sides of the table take turns tapping sugar packets across the table. The idea is to try to get your supply of packets as close to the edge as possible, without going over.

Sugar Pack Hockey.   Players on opposite sides of the table each make a goal with silverware (an open "V" shape). Then they flick a sugar packet along the table top, trying to score a goal.

Sugar may not be great for our kids' teeth, but sugar packets are a great way to pass some meal time!

What if your children suddenly found themselves transported back in time to, say, prehistoric times? Ask how they would:

Find and prepare food. What would your children eat (remind your kids that there were no fast-food restaurants in the Stone Age!)? How would they prepare and eat the food if they didn't have ovens, pots and pans, or dishes?

Make shelter. Where would your kids live? If your children couldn't find a ready-made dwelling, what building materials and tools would they use to build their own?

Communicate with fellow humans. How would your kids convince the locals that they weren't some weird kind of animal, and most importantly, that they were friendly?

Once your kids have thought about what it might be like to live in prehistoric times, pose this question: If you could go back in history and see what life was like thousands of years ago, would you?

OUT AND
ABOUT

This simple game delights the youngest children and makes slightly older kids feel proud that they can play. And it can outlast even the slowest kitchen!

Place several sugar or sweetener packets on the table. Then place a coin underneath one packet. Move the packets around, and see if your child can figure out where the coin is. Or have your child close his or her eyes while you hide the coin. How many guesses will it take to find it?

For added fun, you can maneuver the packets near the edge of the table and drop the coin into your lap. Play up the fact that the coin has apparently vanished—your kids will thrill to be in the presence of a great magician!

After playing this game for the twenty-eighth time, your kids may still be going strong. But *your* eyes may be the ones glued to the kitchen door!

What if it were possible to build a time machine and travel to the past or future? Ask your kids how they would:

Decide which times to visit.   Would it be more fun to visit the past or the future? What would they do once they got there?

Explain their presence.   Would your kids let other people know that they were time travelers? What would the benefits and the dangers be of telling the truth?

Collect data.   What kind of information could your kids gather about other times that would be useful to us now?

Change the past or the future.   If your kids could travel through time, what would they change? What might the consequences of those changes be?

Once your kids have thought about what it might be like to travel through time, pose this question: Would you want to visit the past or the future, if it were possible?

What are people doing in various places of the world as you wait for whatever you're waiting for? That depends on where they're located, of course. See if your child can guess what time it is in the countries listed below, if it is 4 P.M. Eastern Standard Time:

Algiers, Algeria	9 P.M.
Amsterdam, Netherlands	9 P.M.
Bangkok, Thailand	3 A.M. (next day)
Cairo, Egypt	10 P.M.
Canton, China	4 A.M. (next day)
Copenhagen, Denmark	9 P.M.
Galapagos Islands	3 P.M.
Hong Kong	4 A.M. (next day)
Jakarta, Indonesia	3 A.M. (next day)
Khartoum, Sudan	10 P.M.
Melbourne, Australia	7 A.M. (next day)
Moscow, Russia	10 P.M.
Ottawa, Canada	3 P.M.
Reykjavik, Iceland	8 P.M.
Seoul, Korea	5 A.M. (next day)
Tegulcigalpa, Honduras	2 P.M.
Tokyo, Japan	5 A.M. (next day)
Vancouver, Canada	NOON
Zurich, Switzerland	9 P.M.

Wow, just think: If you were halfway around the world, all this waiting would be over and everybody would already be sound asleep!

Maybe you've seen wherever you're going hundreds of times. But have you ever seen it through the eyes of your child? Ask your child to give you a tour while you're walking or driving along; you're sure to see things in a whole new way.

While you're walking, see how closely your child can look at the immediate environment and point out things that make the neighborhood or city unique. Encourage your child to look for the obvious, such as distinctive architecture or statues, as well as the more subtle. The door of the drug store, for example, might have interesting lettering or an unusual frame. Perhaps there's a flower box outside the drug store window filled with exceptionally brightly colored coleus or geraniums. Signs, notices on telephone poles, trees and shrubs, sidewalk benches, utility plate covers, and store names might all be gems waiting to be described.

With your child's keen eye and descriptive powers, your walk can become the adventure of a lifetime!

OUT AND
ABOUT

It's rumored (in our household, anyway), that when Leonardo da Vinci got stuck for artistic inspiration, he occasionally drew a picture upside down. In fact, that may just be why the *Mona Lisa*'s smile looks so weird—she was da Vinci's first attempt at upside-down drawing!

See whether your child can improve upon such primitive artistic efforts by using today's modern drawing tools (paper, pencil, and eraser). Give your child a subject (anything you can view while you're waiting), and see whether your child can draw it from the bottom up. For example, if your child is drawing a person, he or she starts with the model's shoes, moves up to the legs, then the arms, then the torso, then the neck, head, and hair. You might establish other tricky drawing rules, too: Your child draws the right side of the subject and then the left side, or draws the details and then the outlines, and so on. You might be surprised at the results.

So why is the statue of the mayor wearing its hat on its feet? Now, hold on a minute. The paper is upside down!

Waiting Room Scouts

There's probably a lot more going on in the waiting room than first meets the eye. Try this waiting game with your kids and see for yourself how the room is buzzing with activity!

Have your scouts keep track of the subtle activities in the room, in perhaps a five-minute period (you call out "start" and "stop"); how many people come into the room or leave the room, how many times people sit down and stand up, how many times the phone rings, how often someone coughs or sneezes, and so on.

You can add another dimension to the game by having your kids try to predict how many of the events they've been tracking will occur during another five-minute stretch. Whoever comes closest gets to be the timekeeper for the next round.

We can't guess how many of your predictions will be right. But we can predict with certainty that time will fly as your kids watch the door, listen for the phone, and pay attention to life in the waiting room.

A picture might be worth a thousand words, but the place where you and your child are waiting is worth even more!

Choose a part of speech (noun or verb) and see how many words you and your child can come up with that are somehow associated with the place where you're waiting or the event you're anticipating. For example, if you're waiting for a train that will take you to Grandma's house, and the category is nouns, you and your child might compile a list like: Grandma, house, Cleveland, train, station, stop, seat, window, passenger, ticket, conductor, uniform, suitcase, wheels, tracks, scenery, and so on. A verb list might include: visit, travel, bring, ride, hold, sightsee, discover, listen, learn, eat, give, receive, and so on.

So how many words can you think of to describe how it feels to finally arrive? Excitement, happiness . . .

And today's chef's surprise is the noodles with snake toes and broccoli wings, gently broiled at four thousand degrees for six days and served on a lush bed of tree bark!

If your kids are in a silly mood while you're waiting for a meal at a restaurant, let them take turns putting their energy to good use inventing and describing fantasy specials. To make it a team effort, each person adds an ingredient or cooking preparation.

Alternatively, your junior waitpeople can look at the actual menu and offer descriptions (real or imaginary) of each item—the ingredients, how the dish is prepared, its unique nutritional bene-fits, why it's the house special, and so on.

If you have a pad and pencil with you, the waitperson can also take down the orders, noting any special requests for food preparations or sub-stitutions.

And speaking of substitutions, sorry, but there aren't any for the tree bark—that's what makes the dish so rich in Vitamin Z^{48}!

How much does the average bunch of bananas weigh? According to a youngster we know, it weighs in at just under twenty pounds!

You can test your child's knowledge of fruit and vegetable weights (and imagination) during your next supermarket trip. Simply ask your child to guess how much three tomatoes, a pineapple, an eggplant, or another fruit or vegetable purchase might weigh. Then put the item or items you're planning to buy on the scale and see how close your child came.

Another way to play is to tell your child the total weight of a fruit or vegetable that you need, and see whether he or she can guess how many items it will take to make up that amount. For instance, you might say, "We need a pound of onions. How many onions do you think that will be?" When playing with older children, you can relate the questions to some simple math: "The onions cost a dollar for three pounds. How many onions will be a dollar's worth?" See how your kids' produce-shopping skills weigh in!

There's nothing like meeting a famous storybook character to help pass the time while you're waiting. Have your child choose a favorite character from a book you've read together recently and improvise a scene.

Encourage your child to reveal even more about the character than the book does. For example, your child (in character) can tell you how he or she feels about other characters in the story, what life was like before the story started, what his or her plans are, what people in the real world he or she would most like to meet and why, and so on.

You might select another character in the same book and join your child in acting out a scene from the storybook. Or you might improvise a scene that wasn't in the book but should have been, like one in which the wolf tells Red Riding Hood how he's gotten separated from the pack, so Red Riding Hood goes to her grandmother's house to call the Wolf Rescue League!

Here's a game for creating an entire menagerie—with your hands and fingers.

Each child and adult takes turns making animal shapes with his or her hands.

For example, hold your hand sideways, with your thumb pointing straight up. Presto—instant shark! By moving your pinky up and down, you open the shark's mouth.

A few simple changes turns your shark into an alligator. Curl your thumb so your hand is ready for saluting. Hold your hand out sideways. Now, when you separate your ring and middle finger, your alligator will open and close its mouth. Spiders are easy, too—just let your hands crawl across a table.

It's fun to combine your hands with your child's hands to make animals. Or make two animals that can converse with one another—a dog and a horse, for example.

Careful, though—you'll need a zookeeper if you keep this up!

What Doesn't Belong?

Do your younger kids enjoy placing things in categories? If so, they'll like this quick quiz. Read each list to your children, and have them explain why one item doesn't belong.

List 1: tree, flower, rock, grass (The rock doesn't belong because it isn't a plant.)

List 2: fork, potato, ice cream, carrot (A fork is not something to eat, so it doesn't belong.)

List 3: car, bus, chair, bicycle (Everything on this list is a form of transportation except a chair—it just sits there!)

List 4: brother, teacher, sister, father (Teacher doesn't belong—a teacher isn't a family member.)

List 5: red, yellow, paint, blue (Paint may be colorful, but it isn't a color and doesn't belong on this list.)

List 6: table, chair, sofa, bench (You don't sit on the table—it doesn't belong on this list.)

List 7: kitten, bunny, dog, snail (Snails aren't furry!)

If your children find their own reasons to come up with a different answer for any of these lists, all the better!

What Doesn't Belong?   (Older Kids)

Older kids will enjoy testing their understanding of categories and relationships with this quick quiz. To play, read each list to your child and have him or her identify the item that doesn't belong and explain why it doesn't.

List 1: yogurt, milk, peanut butter, ice cream, butter (Peanut butter is the only food listed that is not a dairy product, so it doesn't belong.)

List 2: house, train station, library, grocery store, school (House doesn't belong—it's the only building on the list that people live in.)

List 3: snake, turtle, frog, iguana, alligator (All of these animals are reptiles except the frog, which is an amphibian.)

List 4: bicycle, wagon, scooter, sled, roller skates (All of the toys in this list have wheels except for the sled—it doesn't belong.)

Your children may have their own creative answers for these questions—an independent seven-year-old tester decided that the frog was the odd item on List 3 because, obviously, frogs hop!

What are your family members having for dinner? While you and your family look at your menus, your child can second-guess your orders.

Each family member picks an item from the menu. Then your child guesses which food or beverage each person has chosen. Players might select their favorite foods, in which case, your child's knowledge of family members' tastes will come in handy. Or they might try to trick your child by choosing (at least, for the duration of the game) their least-favorite foods.

To increase the challenge, family members can choose an entire meal—say, an appetizer, vegetable, entree, drink, and dessert instead of an individual item. Your child then tries to guess all of each player's choices. You might assign points to each category, such as one point for guessing the correct appetizer, two points for the vegetable, and so on. Then see how many points your child can rack up for accuracy when players actually order. So who would have guessed that Dad would order the octopus and a side dish of broccoli!

We've all thought it: You're stuck in some kind of difficult situation and you wonder what your favorite person—a friend you admire, even a storybook hero—would do in similar circumstances. The same idea can turn any wait into a game. And when you play in the doctor's office, the game can give your child the encouragement he or she needs to get through an anxious situation.

Here's how to get started. Take quick stock of your surroundings. Are you waiting to see the dentist? Ask your child what he or she thinks his or her favorite storybook character might do if he or she were visiting the dentist. What kind of dentist would Goldilocks visit? And what would the dentist say to Goldilocks? "Somebody's been sitting in my chair and it fits just right!"

What about the doctor? What kind of doctor would Mrs. Sprat visit? What would be her problem? "I just can't seem to lose any weight." "Well," the doctor might say, "have you tried making your dish run away with a spoon?"

Where's the State?

All right, your kids know that Idaho is a state, but do they know where it is? Test their geographic acumen and pass the time with this simple trivia game.

To start, name an area of the country. Your child must then name a state in that area. Say "West," for example, and your kids could say "California" or "Texas." The game also works well with cities, especially capitals.

CALIFORNIA

Try playing the game in reverse. Name a city and see if your kids can name its home state. Or, name a state and see if your kids can name the part of the country where it lies: West, South, North, East.

Older kids can play a more sophisticated version. Name a mountain, river, lake, famous landmark, and so on, then see if your child can tell you what state it's located in. You might be surprised at some of the hidden truths of geography!

Your children are surrounded by gadgets, widgets, and inventions that affect almost everything they do—some very new, and some surprisingly old. Do your kids know when ice cream and bicycles were invented? Test their historical knowledge with this quiz.

Read this list of items to your kids and have them tell you which came first—you can read two at a time, or more for older children. After your children put the list in order, see how close they can come to getting the actual year for each invention.

- modern bicycle—1880
- ice cream—2000 B.C.E.
- Model T Ford—1908
- airplane—1903
- electronic computer—1946
- hot-air balloon—1783
- television—1939
- wheel—about 3000 B.C.E.
- coins—600 B.C.E.
- paper—105

Fascinating—4,000 years of asking "One or two scoops!"

The world of shadows is its own place, where familiar objects like people, houses, and cars take on strange shapes. You and your kids can make that world your own with this playful activity.

The easiest way to play is to have your kids look for shadows on the ground, then associate them with the objects that make the image. This game can get really interesting in the evening hours, when images become elongated because of the low angle of the sun.

Alternatively, let kids make their own shadow theater on the sidewalk. Hands can become animals or machines. Kids can also line up behind one another and make a multi-armed shadow.

Try standing in different places so that the heads of your shadows touch. Move your arms and legs to make a human shadow kaleidoscope—a shadowscope?

You can play these games whenever you have a sunny day and a long walk. After all, you've got to make play while the sun shines!

Pick a door—any door. Right outside your car window, you and your kids will find more doors than you'll ever need to play this quick and easy time passer.

Each player—you and your child, or a group of kids—takes a turn guessing whether a man, woman, boy, or girl will be next to step out of the chosen door.

A variation of this game calls for each player to guess the color of an article of clothing that the next person through the door will wear.

Older kids can also keep score in another variation of this game by giving each color a different value, then taking turns looking at the door. Blue might be worth one point and red worth two, for example.

Finally, each player can guess what kind of clothes the next person out the door will be wearing. This can get pretty wild if someone guesses that "the next person will wear a pink dress," and then a man in a blue suit steps out!

Window Watchers

If it's true that windows reflect the personality of a house, then there are plenty of buildings downtown with enough personality to stock a celebrity parade.

How much personality? To find out, count the windows. Pick a building—any building. Then, select a number of floors and ask your child to tell you how many windows are on those levels. For example, point to a building and ask: "How many windows are on the third, fourth, and fifth floors?"

Young kids will count the windows individually. But you can suggest shortcuts—if there are twelve windows on each floor, and there are three floors, then multiply twelve by three. If your kids don't have any trouble counting the panes, add to the challenge by linking math problems to the total count. For example, you might ask: "All of the windows on the fourth floor minus six is how many?"

Just don't make the math too complicated; otherwise your kids might say this activity is a real pane!

If the waiting room has a window (you might ask the receptionist if a quick trip to a window in the hallway or stairway would be all right), you have everything you need to pass some quality waiting time.

Each person takes turns looking for a certain type of object on the street or sidewalk below, then sees if everyone else can find it: For younger kids, make sure that the chooser gives easy clues, like "I see something red with wheels on it." For an older child, you can be more subtle. If the same car has round lights and a rounded hood, the chooser might say, "I see something shaped like a frog. Its body is the same color as one of the stripes of the American flag, and its feet are made from a substance that grows inside certain rain forest trees."

Make sure that everyone gets a chance to select an object. Before your kids know it, you'll be calling out, "I see somebody waving that it's our turn to go in!"

Festoon, flabbergast, floccinaucinihilipilification. Would your child recognize these as real words? (The last one means to trivialize something.)

Offer your kids a list of words that sound as if they could be made up—like "onomatopoeia" or "cacophonous." Present an equal number that are actually made up, but sound real, like "flontipulate" or "diothonlruling." See if your kids can spot the ringers from the bona fide dictionary entries. (You might want to browse through the dictionary before you leave, or keep a "weird but true" list of words handy for passing the time. Look for entries like "siderdromophobia," which, believe it or not, means a fear of train travel.) Or, you might want to use words from your profession.

As a variation, ask your kids to guess at what the words mean. You're bound to learn some amazing facts—like how "floccinaucinihilipilification" has to do with the process of helping hippos take care of their teeth!

How would your child like the job of cloud designer? What about volcano plumber? Well, both are up for grabs, at least during your waiting time.

Ask your child for some ideas about the zaniest jobs he or she can imagine. For instance, how about Face Painter—his or her job is to decorate people's faces at the coffee shop each morning before they go to work. Then there's Back Scratcher—someone who's always there for others whenever a back itch arises. Perhaps something truly ethereal, like "rain maker," whose duties also include deciding what color the rain (or snow or sleet) will be.

For each "job," have your child suggest appropriate pay (not necessarily cash), the hours of work, the kind of training that would be required, the kind of uniform or gear that would be worn, the dangers, the most gratifying part, and so forth.

Applications are now being accepted for park and playground evaluator. Anyone interested?

Worstest Thing Possible

If the clock hands seem to be weighted down with rocks, try this activity while you wait for your appointment. It's bound to make time speed along as your kids flex their imaginations.

Think of all the possible things that someone might come to the doctor for, then think of which animal would have the worst time of it. Take a runny nose, for instance. That would be something for an elephant! Which animal would be the worst off with a stiff neck? A giraffe certainly wouldn't have fun! Continue the game so that you cover as many animal types as you can think of. Dinosaurs count, too—a T-rex certainly wouldn't appreciate it if he had a sore throat.

You might also imagine what sorts of human treatments would be applied to the animals. A jumbo box of tissues for the elephant with the cold, an extra-long heating pad for the stiff-necked giraffe, and a chair-sized throat lozenge for T-rex.

So you've fallen and skinned your knees—thank goodness you're not a millipede!

It's half-time in the televised First International Waiting Bowl! The cameras are all on your child, who's responsible for providing entertainment and keeping you, the viewer, from switching channels. Suggest the following acts:

Mimes. How about some mime cheers—two, four, six, eight, how long will we have to wait . . . NOT MUCH LONGER!

Commercial Breaks. If you're in the dentist's waiting room, how about launching a new toothpaste? Perhaps your child will play the president of the United States and show off her bright, clean teeth.

News Flashes. What would be so important that it could interrupt a telecast of a national sports event? How about an ostrich that's escaped from the zoo?

PSAs. Offer public service messages to viewers, such as the importance of flossing, eating right, and doing creative activities instead of watching TV—now *that's* public service!

ON THE ROAD

Things to Do Instead of . . .

Handheld Electronic Games

In-car Video

Simple games like concentration are a great way for your kids to pass the time but are difficult to play in a car, train, or plane. Here's a simple portable gameboard to make before you go (see illustration).

To make the board, first cut a ten-inch-square piece of cardboard. Then cut four 10 x 3 3/4 inch strips of construction paper and cover one side with clear adhesive covering. Fold the strips lengthwise with the adhesive covering on the outside, so that one side measures 2 1/2 inches and the other 1 1/4 inches. Next, glue the 2 1/2-inch side to the cardboard. Staple through both sides of the strips and the cardboard at 2-inch intervals to form five pockets on each strip.

To make playing cards, have your children draw pairs of objects on the top half of thirty or so 1 1/2 x 2 1/4 inch pieces of thin cardboard. Or have them find pairs of pictures in magazines and glue them onto the upper portions of the cards. You can cover the cards with clear adhesive covering if you wish. When the preparation is done, pack everything up in a paper or plastic bag, and you're ready to roll.

During your trip you may want to record everyone's impressions and observations (see activities
295–300). You'll be more likely to do this if you
prepare a notebook ahead of time and keep it
handy.

First, purchase a looseleaf binder, ruled paper,
and divider tabs. Then hold a family meeting during which everyone can contribute ideas about
the sections that should be included: weather,
food, buildings, clothing, and so on. When you've
decided on the sections, older kids can label the
divider tabs, and younger children can add appropriate art to the divider pages (pictures cut out
of magazines or drawings of clouds for a climate
section, pictures or drawings of animals for a
wildlife section, and so on).

During the trip, when someone says, "That's
the most beautiful flower I've ever seen!" he or she
will have a section in the notebook in which to
record the memorable sight.

One last thing: Don't forget to pack the book!

Before-You-Go Mileage Bags

Here's a twist on the time-honored practice of giving kids special snacks, small toys, and other diversions as you make your way down the highway: "mileage bags," or goodie bags, dispersed after you have traveled certain predetermined distances.

Have your children help decorate the mileage bags (paper lunch bags, actually). Then, together, decide the distance between goodie distributions, and label the bags accordingly. If, for example, you plan to travel 420 miles and you want to make up five bags, you could have your children label them 70, 140, 210, 280, and 350 miles.

Next, fill the bags with surprises. You can include snacks, small books, small toys, even coupons good for frozen yogurt at the next rest stop. When you're traveling, you'll be all set to give your kids the bags at the designated distances (you can have your children watch highway signs so they can keep track of the miles themselves).

Your kids will be glad to know that while it's twenty miles to the next rest stop, it's only five miles to the next mileage bag!

ON THE
ROAD

Here's a road version of Name That Tune. Before the trip, your child or another family member tapes some songs. Be sure to include tunes that the whole family is familiar with (as a special surprise, you might even want to tape each person's favorite song).

Once you're on the road, designate an emcee to work the tape recorder. He or she says "now" and plays several notes of the first song on the tape. Listeners take turns guessing the name of the melody. The emcee then plays several more notes to verify which, if any, of the guesses are correct. The emcee can continue playing portions of the song until everyone recognizes the song. He or she can then play the rest of the tune (your family can sing along) before the game begins again. Whoever guesses the song correctly gets to emcee the next song.

Doesn't time fly when you're listening to your favorite tunes?

Here's a way you and your children can make a collection of road puppets that will divert your kids' attention from the clock.

Gather the makings of puppets, including old gloves (each cut-off finger becomes a puppet), hollow rubber balls (cut a small hole in each one and poke your finger through the "head"), plastic silverware (draw a face on a spoon), mittens and  socks (move your thumb up and down inside the mitten or sock to make the puppet "talk"), and paper lunch bags (put your hand inside the bottom part of the bag that's folded over and control the "mouth" with your fingers).

To make hats, hair, and costumes for the puppets, use colored paper, contact paper, cotton, yarn, felt, patches, or whatever other sewing and art supplies you have in the house. Add facial features with paint, crayons, or markers.

After you've created the puppets, place them in a shoebox (which your child can decorate) for safekeeping. You might also want to bring along some extra accessories so your puppets can make quick changes en route.

It's a paper holder, a playing board, a felt board, a writing surface, a traveling file, and more! To make a "Swiss Army Notebook" add the following to a smooth-surfaced three-ring binder:

Paper supplies. Include an ample supply of paper: lined, blank, graph, and so on.

Writing and drawing supplies. Punch three holes in a clasp envelope or self-sealing plastic bag to hold pens, pencils, crayons, and markers.

Felt board. Glue a piece of felt to the back of the notebook and cut shapes out of felt scraps to make designs. Store the shapes in an envelope.

Bulldog clip. Attach one to the top of the front cover of the notebook.

Keepsake holders. Add some empty envelopes to store ticket stubs, brochures, and guides.

You may find that this organizer is so handy you'll want one for yourself!

A good basic art kit is second only in importance to the first aid kit. Here's how to assemble one.

First, find a large clasp envelope or a heavy, self-sealing plastic bag to pack the different art supplies in. You will also want to have a case that will protect things and that closes securely. Your stationery or art supply store will probably sell them.

Next, stock the kit with your children's favorite art supplies. Be sure to include basics like crayons or markers, pencils, paper, safety scissors, a glue stick, tape, and a ruler. When you're shopping for the case, you may want to find some new items to add to the kit to surprise your children. Something as simple and inexpensive as a plastic stencil or a French curve will add a whole new dimension to their doodlings.

Finally, if there's room, you may want to include some heavy cardboard to use as a work surface when no desk or table is available.

Now your traveling art kit is ready. All you need are some young artists to use it!

Wouldn't you like to encourage your child to write home to friends and relatives during your trip? A personal letter-writing kit will help him or her to be ready and eager to keep those cards and letters going.

Fill a large clasp or string envelope with the following items:

- an address book, either store-bought or, better yet, one made by your child by folding sheets of construction paper in half and stapling them together on the fold
- a "special" pen or marker; that is, one that goes back in the envelope when it's not being used
- writing paper, envelopes, and postcards
- stamps for both letters and postcards

As you wend your way to your destination, be on the lookout for mailboxes. Unusual postmarks will add interest for friends and family as they receive letters from the road.

While you're at it, we'd really enjoy getting a letter from North Pole, Alaska (yes, there is such a place)!

If you have a pile of junk-mail catalogs and circulars, old magazines and newspapers, plus double-stick tape, drawing paper, and a self-sealing plastic bag, then you have everything you need to make a picture kit for the road.

Gather the printed materials, and your child can help you clip the following types of photos:

People.   Head-and-shoulders or full-length shots of politicians, sports stars, and other interesting individuals.

Scenery and buildings.   Background items such as trees, houses, cars, and skyscrapers.

Miscellaneous objects.   Household appliances, food, toys (look in mail-order catalogues), and other common items.

While your child assembles the kits, you can pack or do other last-minute chores. You can surely picture the benefits of that!

You know that sooner or later you'll hear the dreaded, "Are we there yet?" or "How long until we get there?" How about coming up with some really creative answers for this question in advance, based on your child's own experience? This will help give your child a meaningful sense of time, and provide some amusement as well.

Before you leave, get into the habit of timing the activities that take place during a typical week in your child's life, or jotting down time spans that your child knows, such as the length of classes and sports games.

Include actions such as brushing teeth, getting dressed, eating breakfast, walking to school, doing chores around the house, and walking to a friend's house. Make a list for yourself with the activities and how long they take, but don't tell your child what it's for.

When your list is ready, stash it away with your car supplies. Then, when the infamous question arises, you'll be ready to give some brilliant answers!

A Great Answer

"Are we there yet?"

Younger children often don't have the fine-tuned sense of time required to fully understand a straightforward answer. But if you timed some of your children's familiar activities (see activity 283) before you left, you can offer some interesting equivalencies.

If you don't have prepared times, just use activities you know have set times (classes, sports practices, etc.). First make a list of the activities; then draw a line of boxes next to each entry. Each box represents doing the listed activity once, and the entire line of boxes will represent your total trip time.

Now, when your children ask how long it will be until you arrive, you can have them check off the time you've already traveled in equivalent activities, and they'll be able to relate the time remaining to things they do often.

"Are we there yet?" "No, but it looks like we'll be there in six toothbrushings, one school recess, and three trips to the library."

ON THE
ROAD

Here's a simple word game that puts a new twist on making an alphabetical list of items. The longer the game goes on, the more there is to remember, and the harder it gets.

One player starts by saying a word that starts with A. (You and your children can decide beforehand if you want to limit the choice of words for example, to travel in general, or to the specific kind of traveling you are doing.) The next player repeats the A word, then adds one that starts with B. The third repeats the growing list, then adds a C word, and so on. For example, the first player may say "automobile." Player two might say "automobile, bus." Player three might say "automobile, bus, car," and so on, until the list gets too long to remember.

You can allow players to skip difficult letters like J, Q, X, and Z. And for a variation, have your kids try to do the alphabet backwards.

Now, let's see: What might such a list be like on a plane? How about "airport, blankets, cargo hold, doors, emergency exit, flaps . . . "

Some travelers like to collect souvenir bumper stickers on their journeys. But why not make your own? All the better to remember where you've been on your vacation.

Cut bumper-sticker-sized strips of plain white paper and provide some art supplies. Now your kids are ready to open their own bumper-sticker manufacturing plant.

Each traveler can make his or her own bumper sticker, or teams can work together (for example, one person might draw the pictures while another writes the text). The bumper stickers can include the name of a city, town, or state you're passing through; a logo or design (perhaps an indigenous tree or a house built in the local architectural style); or a slogan (one that says something about the economy, for example).

Who knows? If you pass through any places with exotic names like Essex (Vermont) or Lebanon (New Hampshire), you might even be able to convince your friends back home that you traveled out of the country!

Do your children like secret messages? If so, they can create their own secret codes using the symbols on a road map.

Have your kids start by writing the alphabet down the left side of a page in a single column. Then have them scour a road map and look for symbols to use as replacements for letters. Their selection could be random, or they could try to find symbols to match the letters. For example, an ^ could be used for *A*, @ for *P*, * for *S*, & for *E*, and $ for *I*. Have your kids write the code substitutions to the right of each letter of the alphabet. Once your children have their secret code established, they can write each other cryptic messages.

It's easy to adjust the activity to the age of your children by varying the difficulty of the codes. For beginning readers, you might want to substitute just a letter or two. Older kids may want to try substitutions for the whole alphabet! "*oh—k0^gr@—t t()mO, k @d*!"

Common Threads

If your kids enjoy guessing games, then this activity will probably be a hit with them. The object of the game is to have one person list items that fit an unnamed category and have everyone else try to figure out what the category is.

Let's say that the child giving the clues is thinking of the category "things with wheels." He or she might list "bicycle," "roller skates," "cars," "trucks," "airplanes," and "shopping carts." After each clue is given, everyone gets a chance to guess the category, and the first one to get the right answer goes on to give the next set of clues.

As a variation for older children, you can have players limit their clues to things they see from the car or train that fit the secret category.

OK, what category do these fall under? "Look out the window," "eat at restaurants," "visit museums," "collect seashells," "take day hikes," "play games," and "stay in hotels or motels." Give up? It's "things we like to do on vacation!"

Engage your child in this traveling math challenge to pass the time and distance, at an enjoyable rate!

The game is based on the simple formula Distance = Rate x Time. For example, if you travel at 60 miles per hour for two hours, you will travel 120 miles, because 60 x 2 = 120. (The formula can also be expressed as "Rate = Distance ÷ Time" and "Time = Distance ÷ Rate.")

To play, pose some problems based on your travel speed. For example, ask your child how long it will take to go 150 miles at 50 miles per hour. You can also relate the problems to mileage signs you pass: If your destination city is 90 miles away, how long will it take to get there at 60 miles per hour? For a twist, have your child include the time spent at rest stops to determine your average speed for the trip.

Now when he or she asks "How far is it?" you can answer, "Go figure!"

Dots Away

All you need to play this game is a sheet of paper and a pencil. You can make it as simple or as challenging as you like, and once your kids get started, they can play with each other for miles of smiles.

Make a grid of dots on a piece of paper, either plain or graph. The more dots you place on the grid, the more challenging the game becomes. A good starting size to teach your kids the game is a grid of six dots by six.

The game is played by connecting two adjacent dots with a line. Each player in turn adds a new line to the grid, trying to avoid creating a three-sided box that the other player can "capture" in his or her next move. Every time a player adds a fourth side and closes a box, he or she marks it with his or her initial. Whoever has the most boxes in the end wins.

This could be one time when you actually do want to get yourself into a box!

Here's an activity sure to keep everyone's mind off the time. Write down twenty to thirty place names on small pieces of paper and put them in a small bag. Limit the places to those you will be visiting, or at least driving near, during your trip.

Each child pulls three pieces of paper from the bag and uses a road map to discover the following information about the places named: Which two places are closest together? Which is farthest north? The largest? The smallest? The closest to where you are? The closest to your home town?

After your kids have answered all the questions, have them pick the next three slips of paper from the bag—they can either start fresh with those, or answer the questions again for all six locations.

For a silly twist, you can have them make up their own questions and answers: Which city has the most green cars with orange stripes?

The family that travels together draws a picture together! Place a sheet of paper on a clipboard or other hard surface that can be passed from person to person, and then have passengers take turns drawing. The first artist looks for one item (a barn, river, animal, mountain, bridge, building) in the passing scenery and then sketches it. The next artist spots another object and adds it to the drawing, and so on. Each person should add his or her contribution in such a way that all the objects fit together to create a coherent picture.

For a variation, give each child a piece of paper and have him or her draw a separate picture. Each artist takes turns calling out items that everyone has to include in the drawing. When the pictures are done, pass them around and see just how different they turned out.

There's more than one way to sketch a cow, an ocean, and a Buick in the same drawing!

What's important here isn't what you draw; it's how you draw it. Pass out art supplies or have your kids use their Swiss Army Notebook (see activity 279) to draw the following:

Socks by Sam

One line only. Pick an object you see out the window and draw it without lifting the pencil off the page.

In the dark. Have your children draw with their eyes closed.

Wrong hand. Have your children draw by holding their pencils in the hand they normally don't write or draw with.

Buddy drawings. Have each child start a picture. Call "switch" at regular intervals, and have the artists swap pictures and continue drawing.

Command Performance. With his or her eyes closed, one child follows another child's verbal drawing instructions (draw a circle, a horizontal line, an oval, etc.).

Be sure to keep your children's masterpieces. When you get home, create a Road Art Exhibition and reap the artistic benefits of your industrious trip!

Esrever ni sngis yawhgih daer ot ekil dnuos ti dlouw tahw? Oops! Make that "What would it sound like to read highway signs in reverse?" The answer is clearly, "Pretty silly!" But it makes for a great highway game.

Demonstrate to your children how to read exit signs, billboards, truck lettering, store signs, and anything else they can find, backward. It's easier to start with if they jot down the words on a piece of paper before reading it backwards; then they can try it from memory alone. They'll quickly discover that some of the "words" they come up with may sound like real words.

Once your kids get the hang of the strange pronunciations, they can make the game more interesting by coming up with silly definitions to go with the nonsense words they've discovered. They might just create their own secret language (even if nobody knows what anyone else is saying).

Pay attention: "Daeha sevruc"! And above all, "Pirt ecin a evah."

Even if you've traveled only a short distance, you're bound to notice some differences between your home and your surroundings when you reach your destination. Ask your kids the following kinds of questions as you tour the area.

- How far can you see?
- Is the land flat or hilly? Can you see mountains in the distance?
- What color is the soil?
- Is the air dryer or more humid than at home?
- Is the sky the same color?
- How do sunsets here compare with those at home?
- Does it rain more or less here than at home?
- Does it get dark earlier or later here than at home?

Your children can enter their findings in the Family Book of Observations (see activity 275) or, if they're pre-writers, report them to you or to an older child with writing skills. Be sure to click a few pictures, too. Who, back home, would believe that you could see so far?

Have your children take notice of everyday life in whatever city or town you're visiting; then record what they see in your Family Book of Observations (activity 275). There's sure to be some surprises!

- Do people generally seem more or less hurried than at home?
- How do shopkeepers and store clerks greet you?
- Do you hear any expressions that are new to you?
- Is the accent spoken here different from that at home?
- Do people dress the same here as at home? Are there any articles of clothing unique to the place or culture?
- Are hairstyles similar to or different from those at home? Do men have more or fewer beards and mustaches?

Now here's a real test of regional and cultural differences: Do the people here eat ice cream cones the same way as they do back home?

Travel is an ideal way for your junior naturalists to get a real appreciation for the diversity of plant and animal life. (Stress whatever "no touch" rules you have at home.) Here are some starter questions for your kids to answer in the Family Book of Observations (activity 275):

- Do you recognize any of the trees? Are the trees generally larger or smaller than those at home? Do most of the trees have broad leaves or needles?
- Are hedges common to the area? Do they look like the ones at home?
- Are there more or fewer flowering plants than at home? Do you recognize any of the wildflowers?
- What birds do you see? Do you recognize any of them from home?
- Are there any unusual insects?
- What small mammals do you see?
- Are there deer or other large mammals?

So your youngest child claims to have seen the Loch Ness monster by the sand dunes? Hope that you get all the details for the scientific community!

As you travel about town, have family members consider the architecture they see, noting, for the Family Book of Observations (activity 275), the differences and similarities to the architecture at home:

- What are the houses made out of—brick, wood, stone, stucco?
- Do they tend to be single- or multistory?
- Are there multi-family houses? Are the units side by side or one atop another?
- Are the roofs flat or peaked? If peaked, are they very steep or only slightly angled?
- What are the main colors of the houses?
- Do the houses have porches?
- Where are garages located?
- Are the yards big or small?
- What covers the ground in the front yards— grass, gravel, or plants?
- Where are the mailboxes?

When you get back, your kids will likely have a new awareness of your home and neighborhood, and a new understanding of the phrase, "There's no place like home."

Streets, sidewalks, trees, and fences are some of the things that give each neighborhood its unique feel. As you and your family sightsee and shop, think about these kinds of questions:

- What are the streets and sidewalks made of— brick, asphalt, concrete, or cobblestone?
- Are the streets narrower or wider than those back home?
- Are there parking meters? Does parking time cost the same as back home?
- Where are the street signs—on the corner of a building, on a pole, or built into the curbs?
- What are the fences made of—wood or metal? Are they fancy or plain?
- Are there trees and flower boxes or flower pots along the sidewalks?

One thing is certain: After recording your answers in the Family Book of Observations (see activity 275), your kids will never take the sidewalks for granite again!

Wherever you hail from, your family will no doubt find the downtown area of a new city or town interesting, especially when you compare it to home. Ask your kids questions like these, then log their answers in the Family Book of Observations (see activity 275).

- Are the downtown buildings taller than those at home?
- Are they old or new?
- What are the buildings made of—brick, limestone, glass?
- Do any of the buildings have gargoyles or other decorations?
- Is the city hall similar to the one back home? Would you have recognized it as the town's seat of government?
- Is the main library older or newer than the one in your city or town?
- What are the churches and other religious buildings made of, and are they similar to those where you're from?

How about this one: Once you find the school, see if the playground structures are as much fun as those back home!

Road signs don't just direct or welcome us; they also launch some fun traveling games!

When you spy a road sign that contains the name of a city or state, read it aloud. Fellow passengers then take turns coming up with other cities, states, countries, and continents that begin  with the same letter. For example, suppose you see a sign that reads, "Welcome to Walla Walla." Your traveling companions might suggest Winnipeg, Wisconsin, Waikiki, the West Indies, and so on. Alternatively, players might offer places that begin with the *last* letter of the designated place. When no one can think of any further places that begin with that letter, choose another sign and start all over.

As a variation, you can have each traveler write down a list of all the places they can think of that start with the chosen letter. Players then compare lists and see who thought of the most places, or whose places were the most exotic. You can also up the challenge by adding a time limit.

Did anybody else think of Wessex (an old Anglo-Saxon kingdom in England) or Ahmadabad (a modern-day city in India)?

Follow Me

This map game for kids with reading and arithmetic skills will reveal the best route from A to B and a great way to avoid backseat boredom.

To do this activity, you'll need two copies of the same map, preferably for the area you are driving through. Make sure the maps indicate the miles between cities or towns, or between exits. Give one map to your child and keep one for yourself. Starting at an easy-to-find location (point it out to your child), give travel directions based on the roads, landmarks, intersections, and mileage shown on the map (you might have to point out the mileage numbers on the various road segments).

For example, you might say, "Take I-80 west for fifteen miles; take Route 4 north to the next town; take Route 11 toward the lake for seven miles." Then ask your child where he or she is on the map, and see if you have both "arrived" at the same location!

As a variation, have your child pick the route for you to follow. You can point out a destination on the map and have your child give directions to get there.

Just follow the directions to fun ahead!

Here's a simple word game that's well suited for young readers. It's easy to play anywhere, and it can be put aside and returned to later in the trip.

The object of the game is to write an alphabetical word list (exclusive of particularly tough letters like Q, X, and Z). The first time through the list, every word should be one syllable long. The second time, use only two-syllable words. Third round, the words must be three syllables. The game can be played individually with each player making his or her own list, or as a group collaborating on a single list.

As a variation, you could have your children try to use words relating to things you drive past or actions taking place outside. You could make the game more difficult for older children by not allowing proper nouns and not allowing words to be reused in a different form (for example, if the first list has "take," the second list could not have "taking").

So, ant, apple, antelope, arithmetic—and away we go!

Sometimes a limited view of the big picture can yield hilarious results, as in this guessing game you can play with your child. (For a real-world version of this game, see activity 352).

To play, you cover a picture in a magazine or a book with a sheet of paper or cardboard that blocks out all but a few small sections, then have your child try to guess the big picture.

To create the cover sheet, make a series of uneven folds in a piece of paper, then cut off half-inch pieces along the edges of the folds. When you unfold the paper, it will have holes in it. The fewer holes you make, the more of the picture will be covered. As an alternative, you can make a set of cardboard cover sheets with viewing holes before you leave home. You should make at least three sizes: 3 x 5 inches, 4 x 6 inches, and 8 x 10 inches.

When you're ready to play, simply grab a magazine or book, cover a picture in it, and pass it to your child so that he or she can try to describe the big picture.

Maybe you can't fit a twelve-piece orchestra in your car, but you can certainly enjoy the next-best thing: a set of windshield wipers!

Let the rhythm of the windshield wipers set the pace for a stellar family performance. Each of the passengers chooses a sound: hand clapping, toe tapping, box thumping, or vocalizing a syllable such as "ah," "eee," or "hoo"). You assign each person a time and frequency to make the sound (based on the windshield wipers' rhythm; for example, a "musician" might clap in time to each windshield-wiper beat or tap his or her toe on every other beat).

Each person practices making his or her sound alone; then the whole family performs together. A designated "musician" begins by making a sound. At the signal, the next player jumps in, then the next, and so on, until the entire ensemble is "making music." See how long the family chorus can keep time to the windshield wipers (when players get confused, simply stop the "music" and begin again).

With practice (and a bit of rain), your family members may soon have your car sounding like Symphony Hall!

Sending and receiving postcards is always fun, and the pictures are often a good addition to your own photos of special vacation spots.

You can have your child start his or her own collection of postcards by mailing them home from vacation. Then the cards will be waiting for your child when your family returns, ready to jump-start vacation reminiscing. Your child can write diary-like entries on the postcards, or pretend to be two different people, one sending the card and the other receiving it.

Encourage your child to include a lot of detail on his or her postcards, or to be as silly as possible. After all, he or she doesn't have to worry about confusing the recipient of the cards with comments about the giant squid that visited the harbor featured in the picture on the other side of the card.

If you're traveling with more than one child, you can have them send postcards to each other. But remember, no peeking! The cards can only be read back home.

A popular song once pointed out that "one man's ceiling is another man's floor." In this drawing game, one person's smile may well be another's eyebrows—with hilarious results!

Two people work together to create this top-to-bottom drawing of a person's face. To start, have the two artists sit facing each other with a sheet of paper between them on an armrest or table. Draw a large oval on the page so that the long dimension runs from one artist to the other, then have children take turns adding facial features.

Because each child's view is upside-down in relation to the other's, the features added will take on a different meaning for each child. If one draws a mouth, for example, it may become frown lines from the other child's perspective. In the same way, eyebrows that one child draws could look like bags under the eyes of the other's face. By the time they have completed their drawing, your children will have created two completely different faces. Who knows which is right-side up?

Scavenger hunts are always a lot of fun, but it's impossible to have one on an airplane. Or is it?

Your children can go on an exciting scavenger hunt without ever leaving their seats simply by using the complimentary airline magazines and in-flight catalogs stowed in the seat-back pocket in front of you.

Scan through the magazine and catalog ahead of time and make a list of scavenger-hunt treasure pictures. Pick photographs that lend themselves to interesting clues. A picture of a pool float in a catalog, for example, could be described as "something to keep your head above water," and the clue for a picture of a sandy beach could be "bring a towel and watch out for sea gulls."

When your kids are ready to go on their scavenger hunt, give them each a copy of the magazine or catalog, along with your list of clues, and send them off to find their treasures.

Here's a neat way to get your kids focused on the interesting details at historical sites.

Stop at the information desk on your way in for a map as well as any brochures about special exhibits. Make up a list of things that can be found, then start a group scavenger hunt. You might also want to break up into teams led by an adult or older teenager. To get going, try finding these:

- an unusual architectural detail, such as an ornate drinking fountain, a decorative iron fence, or a stained-glass window
- old-fashioned clothing, cookware, drinking vessels, or musical instruments
- children's toys
- maps from the time period
- the best view of the site or surroundings (is there an observation point?)
- a painting of a child or family life
- things of interest that aren't on the map (exhibits in hallways, pathways, a sundial, a cannon)

How about this one: a hat as old as the one Dad wears while gardening?

What would it be like to live history instead of just seeing it in a museum? The next time your family visits a museum, see whether you can find out.

Look through the museum for displays that might excite your children's imagination. Then ask them a series of questions related to what they are seeing. Frame the queries in terms of what your kids imagine life was like back then, especially for the children of the era.

For example, at an exhibition about the Middle Ages you might ask such questions as: What do you think children wore back then? Where do you think they slept? What foods do you think they ate? What kind of utensils do you think they used, and how are they different from the ones you use? What games do you suppose they played? What types of pets do you think the children had?

If there are guides stationed throughout the exhibition, assign an older child or an adult the task of asking them for the answers to your questions; then compare these answers to your children's.

There's more than one way to look at history!

If your trip includes a stay at a hotel, here's something that turns exploring your surroundings into a fun activity. Set out with your kids in the spirit of exploration to find or count the following kinds of items. (Note: this activity is not intended to be done without supervision.)

- Everything that contains the hotel's logo, from towels to insignias on uniforms
- The number of drinking fountains
- The number of pay telephones
- The number of ice machines
- The highest room number
- The number of "Do Not Disturb" signs on doorknobs
- The number of exit signs
- The combined cost of all items on the restaurant coffee-shop menu
- The number of plants in the lobby
- The number of hotel employees in the lobby at any one time

When you finish this activity, you might want to send the results to the corporate offices. They'd probably appreciate having a group of experts on tap!

How Long Would It Take?

Here's a creative way to get your child's mind off the ride—and flex his or her math muscles while you're at it.

Ask your child how long he or she thinks the trip would take if your family were walking, running, bicycling, on horseback, or in a supersonic plane. For example, if you have one hundred miles to go, walking (at two miles per hour) would take fifty hours to get there (Distance = Rate ÷ Time). Running would be better (twelve miles per hour for a world-class marathoner); you'd arrive in eight hours and twenty minutes. Of course, a horse is faster still (at twenty-five miles per hour).

Don't forget a cheetah (fifty miles per hour), a race car (125 miles per hour), and the Japanese bullet train (250 miles per hour).

If your child is in a real hurry, he or she could travel at the speed of sound (700 miles per hour) and arrive before you could say "Are we there yet?" And for the ultimate trip, traveling at the speed of light (186,000 miles per second), your family would arrive before your child could even think of the question!

With a little imagination and a pencil, the route map in your complimentary airline magazine can become a whole package of games and puzzles (see activity 314 for other ideas). Try engaging your child with these games:

Connect the dots.   Trace selected route lines to create a picture of an animal, person, or thing.

How NOT to get there.   Devise the longest route imaginable to travel from one city to another.

Alphabet tally.   Count all the places on the map whose names begin with the same letter.

You can't get there from here.   Find the two cities that would require the most flight changes to get from one to the other.

By the way, did you know that the *worst* way to get from Bali to Oslo is by way of Yap, Chuuk, Tegucigalpa, and Cleveland?

The route map in your complimentary airline magazine can be a great starting point for all kinds of discussions. Try these topics for starters:

Places you have been. Tell your child about places on the map where you have traveled or lived. Fill him or her in on the climate, any unusual land features, and so on.

What do you know? Engage your child in a conversation about what he or she knows about various places on the map. What do the countries produce? What language do the inhabitants speak? What sorts of foods are eaten there?

Distances. Use examples (such as the distance to the city where Grandma lives) to give your child some perspective about how far different places on the map are from home.

Don't be surprised if, after the first map discussion, you and your child are off on your own imaginary journey!

Here's a vacation pastime that will turn homesick blues (that can pop up even during the most exciting or interesting vacation) into a lively discussion and game.

As you and your family make your way through different places, have your children identify things in their new surroundings that are similar to things at home. They could, for example, find a house that's the same color or architectural style as yours, a street with the same name, familiar stores and businesses, a sign in a store window similar to one at home, a mailbox like yours, or a car or bicycle just like yours. You can have your kids simply announce what they see, or they can make a list to share with everyone else after a set amount of time.

See how many familiar items everyone can come up with, and perhaps take the opportunity to talk about how much you enjoy them at home.

Hey, there's somebody who looks just like Mrs. Jones!

They say that every person has a look-alike. Perhaps the same holds true for cars, minivans, campers, and the like. Can your child find a vehicle on the road that's a clone of yours?

Ask your child to scrutinize the cars, trucks, vans, and other vehicles that you pass. He or she then finds those that are of the same color as your own. Other find-it possibilities include license plates that contain one or more of the same letters or numbers as yours, vehicles that are of the same make or model, and those that contain the same passenger composition (for example, two grownups and one child).

You might set a time limit for each round. Encourage your child to find more blue cars or license plates that contain a Y than he or she did in the previous round. Or challenge your family to a car-search contest: Each participant gets a set amount of time to find cars matching a predetermined list of characteristics (color, number of passengers, etc.), and then see who comes up with the most look-alikes.

Did anyone spot a gray station wagon with two grownups, two kids, and a couple of cats? That's us!

How can you remember the most unusual license plates that you pass on the road? By preserving them in a logbook, of course.

To make a log, use a notebook or sheets of paper that can later be stapled together. At the top of each page write the time span of each license-watch period (say 8:15 to 8:30 A.M.) and the watch category (in this case, out-of-state license plates).

You and your co-travelers scout the road and look for out-of-state license plates. The designated log keeper then makes a list of the license plates as they are spotted.

Your family can also watch for and log other license-plate features, including colors, slogans, and letters and digits (for example, how many license plates can you find that contain the letter W?).

You can reserve a special section in your logbook for vanity plates. See who can find the funniest, most original, or most cryptic in a given time period. Then log the ultimate challenge: the number of license plates each family member can memorize in one sitting.

Look Up!

The night sky at home may be a familiar sight, but how about the stars at your vacation destination?

If you've traveled some distance, see if anyone can pick out some "home" stars on a clear night. Are they in a different spot in the sky? What about the constellations? Are they positioned differently than they are at home? (You might want to make a trip to a bookstore before you go and purchase a stargazing book.)

If you're visiting someone who lives out of the city and therefore away from reflections of buildings and car lights, your kids will probably be amazed at what they can see. Keep their eyes fixed on the heavens and see if anyone can find a shooting star.

You might also take advantage of a brilliant sky and ask your kids to invent a few constellations of their own. With so many stars to see, perhaps your kids will envision a celestial theater inhabited by such notable constellations as the Great Northern Chinchilla and Uncle Jack's Mustache!

This activity will give your kids an opportunity to exercise their cartographic skills and have some fun in the process.

Once your kids have gotten their bearings, ask each family member to draw his or her own map of the place you're visiting. The map should start with the place where you're staying, whether it's a hotel, motel, relative's house, or campsite. Then, based on your comings and goings, see if your kids can expand the map to include nearby roads, buildings, or landmarks that are of importance to them. When the maps are complete, study them to see what was considered worthy of representation.

The maps will serve as a fun record of what is of interest to your children. Should you return to the place, you can pull out the maps beforehand to rekindle fond memories. Be sure to have your kids revise the map when you revisit; the differences will help you chronicle your child's growth. Your kids will also get a chuckle when they see that they chose features such as the "really cool driveway" or the "neat climbing rocks."

Map games are perfect for long car trips. Try these while you make your way toward your first destination.

Hot and cold. Provide a copy of a map and announce that you are trying to get to a certain place. Give a clue, like the first letter of the destination. Your child then gives descriptions like "I'm going west on I–80," to which you reply "hot" if that will lead to the secret destination or "cold" if it leads away.

Map hangman. Select a place on the map and have your kids guess which letters are in the name. If a player guesses a letter correctly, write that letter down on a piece of paper in its appropriate position. If a player guesses an incorrect letter, draw a part of a stick figure. Your kids have to guess all of the letters (or say the name of the place) before the figure is complete. Once they guess the name have them find it on the map.

Now for the greatest challenge: See if any of your kids can refold the map so it fits back in the glove compartment!

After a morning spent at a museum, what did everyone learn? Here's a fun way to find out.

Soon after you've left a museum, or later that day, play a memory game with your family. Take turns describing in detail what you saw. What did you see first? Last? What was your favorite exhibit? The oldest? The biggest? The smallest? The most beautiful? The silliest? The scariest? This is also a perfect time to allow everyone to ask some questions. Did they understand everything they saw? Did it remind them of anything else?

Have a family member write down the answers. You may also want to ask everyone to make some drawings from memory to add to the reminiscences. This museum memory album may just turn into a permanent part of your family's collections.

The smallest thing? How about the ant crawling across the front steps as you went in!

Museum Scavenger Hunt

If you're looking for ways to make museum trips more exciting for your kids, give this activity a try.

First, stop by the information desk and pick up any maps and brochures about the exhibition. Before you set off on the tour, sit down for a moment, look over the materials, and devise a list of five to ten very specific things to hunt for. In a natural-history museum, these could include the T-rex skull, the Atlantic puffin, the trilobite diorama, gypsum needles, and the Audubon print of a giant egret; in an art museum, the list could include a painting of a vase of flowers and a pair of gloves on a table, a sculpture of a child with a bird, a mask from the Aleutian Eskimos, a small gold Mayan figure, a round fan, or "uchiwa," from Japan, and a sculpture of a ballerina with a real net skirt.

Once you've compiled your list, set off for the museum. You can either work together to find all of the items, or you can break into teams with specific assignments.

Perhaps you'll even find a painting of the man who looks like Uncle Fred!

It's fun collecting souvenirs during family trips, but wouldn't you like to encourage your children to find keepsakes other than the typical trinkets that get broken or lost before you get home? For some vacations, especially car trips with plenty of stops at parks and other natural attractions, a traveling nature collection may be just the way for your kids to commemorate their journey. (Note that national parks do not allow collecting. Other parks may have the same rule.)

Anything goes for this souvenir collection, including rocks, pine cones, and twigs. Help your children gather and organize their treasures, and label each with a date and place.

Rocks can be labeled with a laundry marker and kept in a shoebox, while paper tags with strings are perfect for labeling pine cones and twigs.

Pressed leaves can also make great souvenirs. Have your children press the leaves in a notebook between pieces of wax paper, then add written notes about when and where the leaves were found.

When your children get home, not only will they enjoy having added to their nature collection, but they'll be reminded of the fun they had putting it all together.

Navigator's Hat

Even if your children aren't old enough to drive, they can still help get you to your destination. Make (or select) a special hat before you leave home. Then have your kids take turns wearing the hat and performing the following navigator duties:

Sign spotter.   If you're looking for a particular town or exit, or the next rest area, have the navigator watch for signs.

Map travel recorder.   The navigator traces your route on a map with a highlighter pen, adding markers in the appropriate places to indicate all of your stops.

Travel updater.   Have your navigator periodically report which direction you're heading in, how far you've gone, and how many miles you have to travel until the next stop.

And, of course, when you come to a cross-roads and don't have a clue as to where you are, the navigator can help you guess which way to go next!

ON THE
ROAD

Who says you can't hold the Olympics in the backseat of your car? All you need is an odometer!

The driver of the car gives the signal when the odometer reaches a good starting point ("Ready, get set, go!"), then stops the event after a predetermined distance. Try these events to get started:

Numberathon. See who can count the highest in the given time.

Finger exercises. How many times can your children flex their fingers in the given amount of miles?

Heads, shoulders, knees. Have your children touch their own heads, shoulders, and knees as many times as possible in the time span.

By the way, since you're in the car, you can skip the torch-lighting ceremony.

Here's a game that will test your family's memory as well as their powers of imagination.

The first player says, "I see an island, and on that island is . . ." and fills in an object, for instance, "a purple pineapple tree." The second player repeats, "I see an island, and on that island is a purple pineapple tree" and then adds something of his or her own—for example, "a seven-foot-tall pirate." The next player repeats the sentence with the previous items, adds something of his or her own, and so on. See who can remember the longest list and who can contribute the silliest items.

An alternative way to play, especially for older children, is to have all of the items relate to one theme—say, a tropical storm. The list might then include "lemonade rain, sky-splitting thunder, falling blue coconuts, a tent with a leak in it," and so on. When the game is finished, players can tell a story that incorporates all of the items from the memory list. Younger kids can draw a picture of what happens on the imaginary island.

Those coconuts must have been quite a sight!

Lots of books rate places according to economic indicators, housing, and so on. That's important stuff for grownups, but kids have other measures of what makes a town or city good to visit. With this activity, you can begin putting together your "Other Places Rated" book.

The day you leave a town or city, ask your kids to give you their opinions about how kid-friendly the place was, on a scale of one to three, based on:

- Were there many playgrounds or public parks?
- Were there special children's exhibits at museums?
- Were there enough ice-cream stores?
- Did the restaurants offer crayons and activity menus?
- Were there a lot of walls, rocks, or benches to climb on?
- Was there a good place to go swimming?
- Was it a good place to ride bikes?
- Was there a miniature golf course?

So, what do your children think? Was your vacation choice a kid-friendly place?

Pass the Exits

What can travelers do with exit signs besides pass them on the road? Why, remember them, of course!

Appoint a passenger to read and write down exit signs, including names and numbers, as they appear. (This works best with a series of exit signs in close proximity.) Players see whether they can remember and recite the signs—in reverse order.

For example, let's say you've passed three signs. The first player recites the list from memory (for example, "exit 16, Wilson City; exit 15, Clearfield; exit 14, Riverdale"). After passing the next sign, the second player adds, "exit 17, South Sunset," and then recites the other three signs. The next player adds the new sign and recites the other four, and so on, until players can no longer remember the whole list.

Map readers can try this variation. One person identifies the next three exits on the map. Players then memorize the exit names and numbers, and try to recall them *before* the exit sign appears. That's one great way to put your astounding memory on the map!

Palindromes are words or phrases that read the same backward and forward. Some palindromes are both complicated and silly (for instance, "Able was I ere I saw Elba," or "A man, a plan, a canal, Panama!"). There are also plenty of simple words young children can spell that are palindromes.

Have your kids think of as many palindromic words as possible. Some they are likely to know are "mom," "pop," "dad," "tot," "toot," and "noon." Your children can also include names, like Anna, Hannah, and Bob.

As your kids think of palindromes, they can incorporate them into a story (weaving them together with non-palindromes so that the plot makes sense). Try this tale, which begins with two classic palindromes, for starters: "Madam, I'm Adam. Was it a cat I saw? Mom called at noon. She wanted to find dad so they could pop over to the tot lot and toot their horn."

Wow!

Does your child like making and finding patterns? If so, he or she will enjoy this pattern puzzle. It's easy to do, and the results are never the same twice.

Begin the puzzle by drawing a series of simple geometrical shapes on a sheet of paper to create a repetitive pattern. The more shapes you use, the more complicated the pattern can become. It can be as simple as

l o l o l o l o l o

or something more elaborate, like

o o + l o o + l

Now see if your child can figure out the pattern and continue it. For a more challenging puzzle, you and your child can create a two-dimensional pattern, such as

o o

o o

o o

o o

After a while, you and your child will certainly notice another pattern developing: that time flies when you're having fun!

If you've made a Traveling Picture Kit (activity 282), then you have what it takes to instantly entertain all the members of your family. Try these for starters:

Auction.   Select several pictures from the picture bag and auction them off. Give each child an imaginary one hundred dollars. The auctioneer tries to sell each object by describing its artistic merits.

Guess the picture.   One person chooses a picture and gives other passengers clues about its identity. Whoever guesses correctly gets to pick the next picture.

Take and match.   Pass the bag around and have each of your children take a picture from it. Then see if everyone can match his or her picture to something he or she actually saw on the road.

Your children can supplement the picture-kit photos by adding their own drawings, as needed. Isn't it amazing how anyone can draw Snoopy when he or she really needs to?

Puppet Road Shows

If you've made Puppets to Go (activity 278), here are some ideas for performing the best plays on the road:

Coming soon.   Your puppets can rehearse some real-life travel adventures (getting to the hotel, dining with grandparents, touring an amusement park, exploring a zoo). Simply check your agenda, share it with your fellow puppeteers, and rehearse the vacation activities still to come.

Tour guides.   Maybe you don't have friends or relatives who can show you around in each of the cities and towns that you pass, but you surely know some puppets who will take you on a tour. Let the puppets show you the sights as only long-time residents can.

Travel recaps.   How much of your vacation fun can you recall at the end of each day? Puppets can act out the highlights of your adventures and help everyone commit your traveling activities to memory.

Once you and your fellow puppeteers begin, you're sure to discover a trip's worth of great puppet drama!

Luckily, restaurants are becoming more responsive to the needs of families; offerings such as kids' meals and booster chairs are more the rule than the exception these days. Here's a restaurant activity that will also tempt your kids to try new things.

First, equip your reviewers with a notebook set aside for restaurant ratings. You may want to choose a scribe, or you can take turns among older children. Then, after leaving each new restaurant, take a few minutes to write down your family's ratings.

Remind everyone that they are writing the review as if someone had asked his or her advice. Try to answer questions like: "What was the best item on the menu? What was the best thing about the restaurant itself? What was the most unusual item offered?"

Most important, did you get a balloon as you left?

You can always count on airlines to provide you with free reading—and guessing game—materials.

Look through an in-flight magazine (or another publication that a family member has brought along) with your child. Make a list of about ten items for your child to find (don't let him or her see what you're jotting down). For example, you might find a tree, a blue sailboat, a woman with a suitcase, a dog, a man in a suit, an airline pilot, a map, an airplane, and so on.

If you're traveling with more than one child and you only have one copy of the magazine, your kids can work together as a team to find each item. Or, if each child has his or her own copy of the magazine, make separate lists so that your kids can work on the hunt individually.

For an added challenge, put a time limit on the hunting: a set interval of time or a time limit related to an unpredictable event (e.g., the pilot making an announcement).

Oops. Here comes the snack cart now—are your kids ready to hunt down a few peanuts?

Houses, trees, rivers, bridges, cars, trucks. When your children describe what they see from the window, are these the things on the list? Why not get them to look at their surroundings a little differently—say, in terms of circles, squares, and maybe even a trapezoid or two?

To begin this geometry exercise, make a list of basic shapes and forms. You can include circles, squares, rectangles, triangles, ovals, columns, spheres, pyramids, and cubes. Then, have your children look out the car window and try to find one example of every shape on the list. If your children are older, consider eliminating the obvious answers, like wheels.

As your kids get better at seeing geometrically, have them be on the lookout for new shapes to add to their list. They may even want to keep a tally of each type they spot. You can also encourage them to look for shapes within shapes by dissecting what they see: a double window, for example, that is a rectangle made up of two squares.

Well, this is shaping up to be a lot of fun!

Sign Sentences

"Services, Food, Lodging—Next Exit 2 Miles."

How about using those ho-hum words in a sentence, like "Miles was two hours late for school the next day because all the food he ate was lodging in his teeth, and he couldn't get it to exit"?

If you get your children started building sentences from words on road signs, trucks, and billboards, they may not want to stop. And you may hear a lot about this guy Miles by the time you get home.

Encourage your kids to let loose with this game, and have everyone in the car try their creativity with whatever sign strikes his or her fancy. If you want to make it more challenging, have players take turns on whatever words they can spot in a fixed amount of time when it's their turn. Anyone who can use all the words on a sign gets a round of applause.

Hey, Dad, lets keep right on going to the next exit and get five ice-cream cones for Miles and his friends!

"Ensuing egress 5,280 feet." You probably won't see this message on any road sign, but you will, no doubt, encounter the more familiar "Next Exit 1 Mile."

It's great fun to make up fancy renditions of road signs. The more outlandish the better, like "Telecommunications, Sustenance, Bivouacking— Outlet VII" for "Phone, Food, Camping—Exit 7."

Older kids will enjoy making word substitutions for road signs, truck signs, or building signs. The goal is to make the sign as zany as possible, while retaining the original meaning. (It's helpful, though not essential, to bring along a small thesaurus or synonym finder for this activity.)

For a variation, you can reverse this game by making up road signs using complicated words and having your children decipher them. Either way, parental units and offspring will relish a surpassingly diverting recreation!

Singing in the Rain

When is a windshield wiper not a windshield wiper? When it's a metronome! On a rainy day, when your windshield wipers are tapping out their rhythm (WOOSH, woosh, WOOSH, woosh . . .), your family can listen to the "music" and compose a rap song to fit the beat.

Family members take turns contributing lyrics, line by line. These can relate to your destination, rest stops, towns and cities you're passing through, new friends you've made during your travels, relatives you're going to visit, sights you're going to see, passengers you've spotted on the road, or fellow travelers. Since this is a rap song, there's no melody to memorize, which makes it perfect for younger passengers.

Assign a scribe the task of writing down the words and making copies for each family chorus member. Then the choir can perform. Decide how the group should perform the song: all together, or each family member singing one line at a time.

WOOSH, woosh, WOOSH, woosh . . . now, that's a "rap"!

What if your kids patrolled the highways and byways looking for drivers who hadn't brushed their teeth before getting behind the wheel? They'd probably have a blast!

Here's the next best thing, and your kids don't have to unbuckle their seat belts to do it. Just provide art supplies and paper, and suggest that they make up their own tickets listing silly fines and violations, like the following: fine for driving with a cluttered glove compartment—$5,000; sitting in a standing-only zone—$50; parking on top of a bus—pay seventeen doughnuts; fine for ruining rain drops with windshield wipers—$3 million.

You can also have your children make up some silly excuses to give to a trooper. "Gee, officer, I'm sorry, but the hamsters in the glove compartment were restless," or "But officer . . . I didn't know I couldn't park my car on the steps." Then there's always this one: "I'm sorry the car was shaking but we were all just laughing so hard!"

Snork!

Here's a great car game that can easily be adjusted to the ages and skills of your children. The point of the game is to have everyone try to guess the identity of an object while one person supplies clues.

To play, one person picks an object that you pass frequently, such as a signpost, a green car, a gas station. Then, each time the car passes a matching object, he or she calls out "snork" (or some other nonsense word). Everyone else tries to figure out what the item is by looking around when they hear the word "snork" and taking a guess.

To increase the challenge, you can make the object very specific. For example, instead of a green car, the person may pick a green car with four people in it that's traveling in the opposite direction. Then, when someone makes a partially correct guess, the chooser can let the guesser know that the answer is close, but not close enough.

The game can also be varied by picking items that come up more or less frequently. But, be careful. If someone picks fence posts, it may all come down to "Snork, snork, snork, snork, snork . . . "

Onomatopoeia is a term for words that sound like what they are, such as "buzz," "hiss," and "ping." With a little applied theatrics, your kids can probably make a lot of words onomatopoetic.

The word "big," for example, which even though it isn't (big, that is) can certainly sound "big" if said in a deep, resonant voice. And even though "little" is bigger than "big," it won't sound that way if it's said in a soft, squeaky voice.

Make a game out of creating sentences that use words that sound like what they describe, and challenge your kids to use as much tone, volume, and inflection as necessary to take the idea to a silly extreme.

Begin by helping them think of words that genuinely fit the bill: "hiss," "buzz," "crunch," "pop," "sizzle," "bang," and "swish," for example. Then have your children add their own interpretations of how particular words should sound.

So, what's the sound of children pretending to be asleep in the backseat of a car? Snoooooooze!

Start–Stop–Guess

Do your children know how far a mile is? Can they relate that to how fast your car is traveling or how long it takes to get where you're going? Here's a simple car game that will hone your kids' skills for estimating distances.

The object of the game is to guess how far your car has traveled in a given amount of time. When all the players are ready, the driver says "start" and checks the odometer. After a short while, he or she says "stop" and checks the odometer again. Each child then states his or her guess as to how far the car has traveled in the elapsed time.

After you've tried this once or twice, have your children count to themselves from the beginning to the end of a measured mile. Then try the game again with random distances and see if their guesstimates have improved. As a variation, you can have your children take turns issuing the start and stop commands, or have them call out when they think a specified distance has been traveled.

Now when your kids ask, "How far is it?" you can have them take their own best guesses.

If you and your co-travelers can't get off at every train stop and explore, why not at least take some imaginary excursions?

In this activity, your child tells you what your family would see and do if they were getting off at the next stop. If the train stops at a place where your child has been, he or she can describe the trip from memory (including streets, buildings, museums, and restaurants). Otherwise, your child can detail an imaginary route, inventing names of places you might go, people you might meet, and so on.

Alternatively, your child might pretend that the train can stop anywhere in the universe—a distant country, continent, or even planet. He or she can describe the weather, food, houses, and other things that the family will see after stepping off the train. Your child can even create a pretend itinerary detailing the tourist attractions the family will visit (perhaps the Milky Way Planetarium or the Martian Wax Museum).

Next stop, anywhere in the world!

Trained Guesses

A train trip is a nice change from car travel for your family; there's always lots to see and plenty going on close at hand. Why not play this game to get your kids guessing about the trip and observing more at the same time?

To play, you ask your children questions relating to the trip, and they try to guess the answers. Then have everyone watch for the right answer. After a few questions and guesses, your kids will probably want to ask questions, too. Here are some sample questions:

* How long until the next station?
* How many cars will be waiting at the next crossing?
* How soon until another train passes going the other way?
* How many minutes before the conductor comes back into this car?

If you have older children, put them in charge of writing down the questions and guesses. And look for opportunities to ask your children more questions about their guesses. Before you know it, they'll be experts at rail travel!

Wouldn't it be convenient to have a "getting there" and "getting home" picture record, all on one sheet of paper? Your child will only need art supplies and a piece of paper—the largest that can be conveniently used while en route.

Have your child look out the window and find something interesting: an unusual house or building or car, a cloud formation that looks like an animal, or a mountain, beach, lake, or pasture. He or she then draws it in on one small area of the paper. When the scenery changes, your child adds another drawing near the first one. So the travel collage might start off showing your city or town, change to rural or farm country, then gradually show a city rising on the horizon, and culminate with a bustling downtown area.

If several artists have created collages, when you get home, you can tape the pieces of paper together and create a wall display. Now *that* will really capture the trip in a way no camera could ever do!

Travel Tally

If your children are entertained by counting things along the highway or rail tracks but are bored with the usual categories of trucks, buses, and license plates from home, try this twist for some variety.

To get your children started, give them some unusual categories of things they can count and have them keep a tally on a piece of paper. You might include silly categories, such as cars driven by men with mustaches, or elaborate ones, like trucks with red lettering going downhill.

You might also try having your children tally items by color, by size ("smaller than the car," "bigger than the car," or "bigger than a truck"), or by building type (restaurants, gas stations, office buildings, etc.).

Depending on the region you're passing through, you may want to limit the viewing area so your children can keep up with the tally. But remember, accuracy doesn't count nearly as much as fun!

Wouldn't it be great if you and your co-travelers could find some hidden treasures?

Make a list of "treasures" you know you'll be passing on your journey: expansion bridges, parks, and so on. If you've taken the route before, you can be specific, listing the name of a restaurant or a hotel. Otherwise, you can note general items, such as "a tall building in Chicago" or "a farm on Interstate 93." Give each participant a copy of the list. Older treasure seekers can check off found objects and help younger players to do the same.

You can plan long-term treasure hunts that will take the whole journey to complete (the final object on the list might be "grandma's house" or "the sign outside your hotel"). Or you can plan a series of treasure hunts using the same list, with such items as "the next exit sign," "the first restaurant we come to," and "a rest stop."

Here's hoping that you won't have to use your treasure-hunting skills to find your child's favorite baseball cap along the way!

When the miles get monotonous, pull out the Card-Game Board (activity 274) you made before you left home, and pass the time with some new twists on old favorites.

Highway lotto. Fill the game board pockets with cards placed face up. Every time someone spots something outside the window that matches the image on one of the cards, remove that card. The object of the game is to remove all of the cards in a specified amount of time or by a specified distance.

Highway bingo. To start the game, place the cards in the pockets face up. Every time one of the objects is spotted, turn that card over. Players try to get a complete row or column in the shortest time possible, then call "bingo!" (or a term of your own choosing).

While you've got the game board out, see if your kids can invent their own games. When you get back home, you might even be able to market them and pay for a few future vacations.

Passing notes may not be tolerated in class, but in a car, plane, boat, or train it can be a fun way to pass the time.

Your children can write notes to you, each other, imaginary friends, or famous people they'd like to meet along the way. Here are some starter ideas:

Fortune cookies. "You will take a long car journey to mysterious places."

Travel alerts. "Watch for Falling Bananas" or "Caution: Giant Cicada Crossing Ahead."

Greeting cards. "Congratulations on passing mile marker 156 without a rest stop."

Notes to famous people. "Dear President Lincoln, Why are you hanging out on that mountain with those other three guys?"

Just plain silly. "Don't look now, but there's a slice of apple pie on your head."

Your children can address the notes to other family members, or you can put them in a paper bag and one person can read them aloud.

Here's a note you may well see: "Dad, let's stop for ice cream at the next exit!"

Traveling Shuffle Story

Your family has been driving for three hours, and you still have 150 miles to cover today. Or perhaps the ferry's been out at sea for a bit longer than your kids' patience can tolerate.

For this activity, you'll need pictures from magazines and catalogs. Shuffle the pictures and give one of your children the top picture from the stack. Then have him or her use the subject of the picture, along with something he or she can spot on the horizon or along the highway, to make up a story. If the first picture features a dog, for example, and you are driving past a shopping center, the story might begin, "One day, Dorothy the dog went to the supermarket to buy some bananas." Then give the second picture to the next player and have him or her continue the story: "Along the way, she had to stop at the tollbooth and threw her toothbrush out the . . . "

Hopefully, your story won't go to the dogs!

When you're traveling, familiar things can often take on a new look. Your children's favorite picture book certainly will if you try this storytelling twist.

Before you head out on your trip, select a few of your children's favorite picture storybooks that have short text. Copy the text, and when you need entertainment, announce: "We're going to create a new story!" Don't tell your kids the title of the book. Then page through your copies of the text and find words to replace. (Common nouns or action verbs work best.)

For each replacement, ask your children for a word in a particular category—an object, an animal, or an action—and have them name something they can spot from the car or train window. Write the replacement word in your copy of the text. When you've gone all the way through the story, read it aloud and be ready for the laughs!

And so, with apologies to Margaret Wise Brown, "In the great green room there was a cement mixer, and a red guardrail and a picture of the cow jumping over the police car . . . "

The changing world outside the window of a car or train provides a lot of things for your child to look at. This activity will enable him or her to get a different view of the scenery.

To play, all your child needs is a rolled-up piece of paper or a cardboard paper towel or toilet paper tube. Your child places the tube up to one eye, closes the other, and watches the passing scenery for a short amount of time (one minute is plenty). Then the child describes what he or she saw in as much detail as possible, based on the view through the tube. You might need to ask some questions to get the descriptions rolling, such as, "Did you see the red house?" You can also ask questions about things that weren't there—like a brown cow—and listen to the detailed descriptions of the phantom animal!

As a variation, have your child provide a running commentary as he or she watches the passing scenery through the tube. You can also vary the game by limiting how much the tube can be moved around. It will be a fun challenge for your child to describe unfamiliar territory from a decidedly narrow view.

Here's a memory game that your family can play while traveling in any kind of vehicle, because the vehicle itself becomes part of the game!

Begin by saying, "The car (or train or plane or boat) went . . ." Then have your children string together prepositional phrases. For instance, your child might say, "The car went through the mud." The next player repeats the sentence and adds a new phrase, such as "under the bridge." Each child in turn repeats the previous sentences and adds a phrase of his or her own.

If your kids are describing the car, they might end up with something like this:

The car went under a trestle, through a tunnel, over a bridge, around a curve, past a mountain, across a line, beneath a cloud, into a tollbooth, up a ramp, down a hill, out of town . . .

Keep going until the string gets too long to remember. The sentence about the car could conclude, "and finally to Grandma's house!"

Vanity, thy name is license plates—if they're custom-designed by you and your fellow travelers.

Put your co-passengers to work creating vanity plates for cars, trucks, buses, bicycles, and other vehicles that you pass on the road. The plate might relate to the model or make of the vehicle, weather conditions, where you are, and so on. For example, "2COOL" might be the perfect plate for a convertible, especially if it's a windy day. And "PREZ" might be an appropriate license plate for an important-looking car you pass in Washington, D.C.

See whether family members can reach a consensus on the ideal vanity plate for each vehicle, or you can "attach" several plates to the same vehicle. Then, the vanity-plate creator draws a picture of the vehicle with its new vanity plate.

Alternatively, you can list vanity-plate slogans beforehand, either on the road or before leaving home, and search for a vehicle that's worthy of bearing each plate. How long will it take to spot a car that you can designate "NO1AUTO"?

ON THE ROAD

Bringing out the video camera when you're traveling will not only relieve the boredom of a long drive or ride, but it will provide you with some unusual video memories of the journey. Be sure to include the little things as well as the big events. For instance:

On the road.   Give each family member a chance to be on camera and describe the area you're traveling through.

Tour of the car.   Since you're spending so much time in the car, why not feature the vehicle in a video segment.

Stocking up.   Have your kids describe the special attractions of gas stations and rest stops.

By now your family video trip record is growing! (See activity 356 for more video ideas once you return home.)

A video camera is a great way to record impressions, thoughts, and feelings about your trip once you're back home. Try these starter ideas:

Welcome home.   Catch your children on video as they rediscover their house, pets, yard, and toys. Then play the tape back. Your kids may be surprised to see how happy they look to be back home again.

Interviews.   Give each member of your family a chance to talk about his or her favorite parts of the trip. You can enlist your older children to conduct interviews and do the camera work.

Treasure hunters.   Have your children describe the treasures they brought back with them.

Finally, be sure to have a family film festival a month or so after the vacation. Your children can wear their favorite souvenir T-shirts from the trip, and you can plan a dinner menu featuring foods from the places you visited. Then settle down, pop some popcorn, and roll the video for everyone to enjoy!

Need some quieter time while you're traveling, or perhaps a challenging game with a different slant? Then try this.

Assign someone the role of "it." That person tries to make another person say something. Depending on the age of the players, this may be relatively easy—perhaps asking a young child a simple yes-or-no question. For older players, it might take some ingenuity: "it" can ask questions nonchalantly like, "Anyone see that thing that just flew in the window?"

If ingenuity doesn't have the desired effect, perhaps some tall tales will. The person who is "it" can simply take advantage of the opportunity to spin endless, pointless yarns without interruption. That's sure to make someone crack!

Alternatively, make the object of the game to get someone to laugh by telling jokes, making funny faces, or asking silly questions. You and your family will probably find it almost impossible to refrain from laughing when the goal is to be serious. Now what's so funny about being on vacation?

What's Behind the Tray?

Kids love guessing games, especially if you can add a note of suspense by hiding the answer in an interesting spot. Your younger child will likely enjoy this airplane guessing game—it uses in-flight magazines to provide the mystery objects and the seat-back tray in front of you to conceal the answer until it's time to reveal it!

Start by finding a picture in the magazine or catalogue that lends itself well to clues that your child will understand. A picture of a car, for example, can be hinted at by saying, "We have one at home; it's something with wheels; it has four doors;" and so on. Fold the magazine so that your choice faces out (or tear out that page), put it on the tray, and fold up the tray.

After a predetermined amount of hints and guesses, or when your child gets the right answers, flip the catch, plop the tray down (assuming the flight attendants haven't instructed you to put it in the upright position), and Taaa-Daaa—there's the answer!

What child isn't fascinated by the big trucks on the highway? Here's a simple way to parlay that interest into a fun activity that will help pass some time on the interstate.

First, have your children come up with a list of things trucks carry. The items on their list can be general or specific. The list could, for example, include "food" as well as "potato chips," or "construction materials" and "pipes."

As your children come up with items for the list, you or an older child can write them down, leaving room next to each entry to tally sightings. Then, have your children pick a time or distance at which to stop counting—say, twenty minutes or twenty-five miles (or, to add an element of the unknown, "at the third exit sign"). When everyone's ready, announce that you'll start counting in one minute (or one mile), and then see how many trucks your children can find that match their cargo list. They may also want to add new items to the list as they go along.

Let's see, that's three milk trucks, five moving vans, and one truck full of popcorn. Right?

Who's on Board?

With lots of stops and people getting on and off, determining who's on a train can be as interesting to your children as what's outside the window.

Have your children start a "Who's on Board" tally as soon as you're settled on the train. First, help them select a set of statistics to track. For example: How many people are in this train car; how many of them are girls, boys, women, men, how many people are traveling alone; how many people get on or off at each stop?

When your kids have their list of "demographic" questions, have them make a grid on a piece of paper to record the answers; it can show categories across the top and stops down the left margin. Then, have them tally and record the information at each stop the train makes. They can compare the different stops, noting which is the busiest, which is the quietest, and so on. For a variation, your kids can try to guess where certain people will get off the train. All aboard!

Have your kids take a look around at their fellow passengers in the train or airplane. Now have your kids close their eyes and ask them the following types of questions:

- How many people are in the train car or plane?
- How many of them are children?
- How many passengers are working or reading?
- How many people are wearing something blue?

Add your own people-related questions that are appropriate to your mode of travel. For example, if you're riding in a train and have to travel the aisle on the way to the bathroom, you might ask your child: How many people are sitting on the right side? How many people are snoozing? How many passengers are eating?

Who knows? You might recall some of your fellow passengers as vividly as you do your vacation!

Word Family Game

This game may be tame, but it's not the same as one that's lame. Your kids won't shun this fun in the sun or on the run. In fact, they may stop whining, drop what they're doing, and hop to attention.

To play, have your kids try to make a sentence using four words from a "word family" (a group of words that share beginnings or endings). For example:

- The mole in the hole stole a pole.
- The cat spat at the rat.
- The big rigs haul twigs and figs.
- The thin pin is in the bin.

Other word families your kids can use are those that end with -an, -at, -it, -et, -ug, -en, -og, -op, -un, -ame, -ind, -ine, and -ing, to name a few.

As your kids get good at making up these silly sentences, have them try for more than four words in each. And, of course, humor counts!

So, hug a bug and lug a rug; scan the plan to man the flan; this quiz has a quiet quality that will quadruple your quotient of quick entertainment.

Here are four word games you can do with a homemade game board (see activity 274). (Instead of affixing pictures to the cards, write letters on them.)

Hidden words. Place the letters in pockets to make words horizontally, vertically, and diagonally, then cover the letters with the other game cards. Take turns uncovering and recovering a single letter. When someone thinks he or she knows the location of an entire word, that person can uncover all of the letters in that word.

Rows and Columns. Randomly place letters on the board and take turns forming as many words as possible with the letters in a single row or column. Set a time limit or use the car's odometer.

Quick spell. Place all of the letters facedown on the board, then pick one at random for each child's turn. That player then has to find an object that begins with that letter and spell it.

Don't hesitate to make up your own word games, too. No one will get bored with this board!

You can use the complimentary in-flight magazine on a plane or any other magazine to play a simple word-puzzle game with your older kids. Here's how. First, browse through the magazine and look for interesting pictures and phrases. These can include pictures of animals, people, or cars, and descriptive words used in advertising copy.

Next, concoct a sentence in your head by combining the pictures and words. If, for example, you found a picture of a bear and one of a fish and the phrase "outrageously delicious," you might turn them into the sentence, "The bear ate the fish and said it was delicious."

Write down the sentence, leaving blanks for the pictures and words you found (in this case, bear, fish, and delicious). Below each blank, write a clue for the picture or phrase (for example, "a big, brown animal," "a great swimmer," and "tastes fabulous"). You can also include the page number.

Then hand the magazine and sentence puzzle to your children, and see how quickly they can fill in the blanks. Perhaps they will be inspired to make a puzzle for you!

It's *Smith Trek*, and the mission is to go where no family has ever gone before!

No, this isn't a new TV show—at least not in the conventional sense. The idea behind this activity is to have your children produce their own "television" show using a large box (you can often get one from an appliance store) from which you've cut out a screen and added a dial or two (yogurt-container tops affixed with brads). If you can't get a box, you can make a cardboard television facade with a large piece of posterboard.

Your kids can do on-location interviews, with the interviewee wearing beach clothes or a hat representative of one of the places you visited. He or she might also explain how certain foreign foods should be cooked or describe customs the family encountered in other parts of the world.

Or how about this one: your children can advise other kids on the best way to keep occupied while on the road. Take notes; you'll learn a lot for the next time you travel!